TURKISH CUISINE

TURKISH CUISINE

Published and distributed by

Mert Basım Yayıncılık Dağıtım
Ve Reklamcılık Tic. Ltd. Şti.

Photos:
Nadir Ede

Layout:
Fatih M. Durmuş • Kemal Özdemir

Typesetting:
AS & 64 Ltd. Şti

Printed in Turkey by

ISBN 975-285-114-2

MERT BASIM YAYINCILIK DAĞITIM
VE REKLAMCILIK TİC. LTD. ŞTİ.

Seyrantepe Mah. Altınay Cad. Gül Sok. No: 13/4
Seyrantepe/İSTANBUL
Tel: (0212) 321 72 63 - 64 - 65
Fax: (0212) 321 72 66
mertbasim@superonline.com.tr

TURKISH
CUISINE

TUĞRUL ŞAVKAY

TURKISH CUISINE

Anatolia was the host of many civilisations such as Lycians and Hittites and lastly has been the host of Turks, who immigrated from Central Asia. The culture of nomadic Turks combined with the settled culture of Romans and blended with Egypt, Syria, Iran, Iraq, Balcans and the Aegean to make up today's Turkish culture. Naturally this multi cultured framework shapes life and art in Turkey. While investigating Turkish cuisine, bearing multi culturedness and regional differences in mind would be of great help in understanding.

Eating plays an important role in Turkish peoples' lives. Especially dinner is a social occasion where all family members enjoy being together and have a chat. The oldest member starts the meal, others are to follow and so show their respect. Everybody must be considerate and respectful. If the meal is served on a single plate instead of individual plates, members are supposed to eat just what they have in front of them. There are irreplacable favourites in the Turkish cuisine, such as:

Eggplant:

With nearly fourty different varieties of cooking, it is also admired by the foreigners. Its nicotin content supplies a spicy taste.

Yoghurt:

Yoghurt is eaten in almost every meal. Added into dishes during or after cooking, it is used lavishly. With the addition of water it is turned into ayran or eaten plain. In cases of toxication, it is advised to eat yoghurt known to possess anti toxic properties.

Pickled Vegetables:

Almost all vegetables, and even anchovies may be pickled. During winter when fresh vegetables are not abundant, pickled ones are used as a substitute for salad. They are necessarily eaten with dried beans and pilaf.

White Cheese:

Known worldwide as fetta cheese, the name given by the Greeks, white cheese is produced all around Turkey with regional differences resulting from salt-fat content, fermentation period, taste and texture. Any breakfast can not be considered without it and it is used in böreks and mezes.

Olives:

Both the green and a little more matured black types are eaten amply at breakfast served with a mixture of olive oil, oregano and red pepper into which toasted breads are dipped.

Onion:

The white, red, fresh or dried types are consumed lavishly. It is used in nearly all hot or cold dishes.

A typical Turkish breakfast consists of white cheese, olives, jams, butter. eggs, sucuk (spicy charcuterie), bread and tea.

There is a tradition to prepare summer's ample variety of fresh produce for winter. Methods for winter preperation are; drying fruits, making jam and compotes, pickling vegetables, cooking pekmez from grape juice, making tarhana, yufka and tomato paste.

Dishes are generally cooked in liquid thereby eliminating the necessity to use sauces. Meat, grains and vegetables are cooked in the same pot, enhancing the flavour and taste of the dish, lid of the pot closed.

Dolmas-stuffed vegetables have a great part in Turkish cookery. Vine leaves, peppers, eggplants, mackerel and mussel may be stuffed. Two kinds of stuffing are with minced meat or with rice, which constitutes a surprising example by combining currants, pinenuts, sugar, herbs and spices. Turkish cuisine is colorful and multi cultural.

Turkish Coffee

Adana Kebap

Salads and Mezes

Although there is a conflict in Turkish Cuisine as to which dishes are mezes and which are salads, there is one fact admitted by everybody: rakı is served with mezes and salads. All fermented alcoholic drinks, including are is prohibited by Islam. Therefore, Turks, after settling in Anatolia, have never made use of delicious grapes grown, by producing wine. However, a combination of grape and anise was distilled to produce rakı whose production was then widespread and improved as an alternative to wine. During the reign of Ottomans, rakı was drunk just by men, who were accompanied by lute playing and singing ladies. Rakı, served with two separate glasses, one for the spirit, one for water, used to

be drunk with delicious and charming mezes. Rakı tables were addresses where men enjoyed good music and good talk. If men preferred to drink with friends, they went to meyhanes, restaurants serving only rakı, meze and salad, sitting on short stalls around a short table chatting and improving their friendship, while tasting numerous and mouth-watering mezes. In Turkey, politics and arts are discussed on rakı tables similar to cafes in France. After the establishment of the republic in Turkey, the system of new government was decided at rakı tables of Atatürk. Nowadays meyhanes are also frequented by women and the tradition of serving numerous varieties of mezes and salads in small cups, presented on a large tray still continues. The purpose of eating meze is not to make the stomach full, but to ease the drinking of rakı and to tickle the palate.

In serving meze, variety is more valued than harmony; hot, sweet, salty and sour varieties are in unity. Small böreks are served hot, whereas salads and mezes in oliveoil are served cold. The only common point of mezes is that all varieties are delicious and attractive.

Salads and mezes are eaten nearly in all the meals also without rakı as the main course or as the accompanier of main dishes. We can say that the only sauce for salads is made of oliveoil, lemon juice or vinegar and salt which is used lavishly on any kind of vegetable according to the season and the tastes and preferences of the lady preparing it. The only exception to this light sauce is the yoghurt sauce consisting of yoghurt, oliveoil, garlic and salt usually poured over charcoaled or fried vegetables. "I wish I were a fish in a bottle of rakı." Line of the famous poet Orhan Veli simply summarises the passion of Turkish people for rakı and the rakı table and mezes and salads.

SHEPHERD'S SALAD
ÇOBAN SALATASI

for 10 persons

1 kg Medium sized tomatos
500 gr. medium sized cucumbers
5 green peppers
5 dried onions
1/2 bunch parsley
4 small red radishes

For the sauce:
1 cup olive oil
1 table spoon vinegar
salt

PREPARATİON

Peel the tomatos, remove the seeds and cut them in small chunks. Remove seeds of green peppers and cut them in cubes. Slice the dry onions without their peels. Peel the cucumbers, cut them into four diagonal pieces and then slice them. Cut the parsley leaves and put them in a salad bowl together, and mix them. Pour the stirred sauce and serve on green salad leaves.

PICKLED CUCUMBERS
SALATALIK TURŞUSU

5 kg. cucumbers
1/2 bunch dill
1 branch for evey 2 kg. jars fennel
1 tea spoon salt
1 clove garlic
2 red peppers
2 bay leaves

for the pickring juice:
300 gr. salt
20 cups water
800 gr. vinegar
25 gr. salts of lemon
1/4 tea spoon turmeric
1 tea spoon mustard powder
2 clauks
1 table spoon allspice

PREPARATION

Pierce the cucumbers with a pin, wash and place in the jars. Add the dill, fennel, bayleaf red pepper and garlic on top of the cucumbers. Place the salt, water, vinegar, salts of lemon, turmeric, powdered mustard, clove and allspice in a saucepan and boil. Pour the pickling juice into the jars and cover. Rest for 10 days at room temperature and serve.

P.S. You can prepare the pickled green pepper and the pickled cabbage in the same manner.

Eggplant Salad
Patlican Salatasi

<u>for 10 persons</u>

<u>2 kg. medium sized eggplants</u>
<u>2 medium sized lemons</u>
<u>1 cup olive oil</u>
<u>salt</u>
<u>2 cloves garlic, crushed</u>
<u>2 cups yoghurt</u>

To Garnish:
<u>1 tomato</u>
<u>1 green bell pepper</u>
<u>1/2 cup parsley, chopped</u>
<u>6 black olives</u>

PREPARATION

Pierce the eggplants with a fork, place in a pan over an open flame or on a high gas flame or on charcoal and cook for half an hour, turning often until the skin blisters on all sides and the eggplants become soft.

Once the eggplant is cooled down, cut lengthways into two. Scoop out the pulp, sqeeze out all the moister and mash with a fork on a wooden board. Place the eggplant pulp into a bowl and add the lemon juice, olive oil, salt, garlic and yogurt. Mash until it becomes a puree.

Place on a serving bowl and garnish with tomato, bell pepper, parsley and black olives. Chill for half an hour before serving.

WHITE BEAN SALAD
PİYAZ

10 persons

500 gr. white beans
4 medium sized tomatoes
1 bunch parsley
3 dry onions, medium
salt
1 teaspoon rad pepper
4 eggs
black olives

for the dressing:
1/2 cup olive oil
1 tea spon vinegar
1/4 lemon juice
salt

PREPARATION

Wash the beans and soak in cold water over-night. Cover with cold water and put on to boil. When boiling, remove from heat and leave aside. Return beans to the boil in their soaking water, simmer gently over low heat until tender but still intact. Add salt to taste after 1 1/2 hours cooking. When tender, drain and place the beans in a bowl.
Crush onions with a little salt. Then slice thinly into semicircles. Add to hot beans with lemon juice, vinegar and combined oils. Add the chopped herbes and chill salad for 1-2 hours.
Serve in a deep bowl. Garnish with sliced green pepper and quartered hard-boiled eggs. Wash and chop the parsleys and save a little for later. Boil the eggs and cut them into 4 pieces or slices when cool. Stir the dressing in a bowl and pour on the beans. Add the dry onions, sliced parsley and part of the tomatoes and stir. Decorate the piyaz with the rest of the tomatoes, egg slices black olives and parsley.

ALBANIAN LIVER
ARNAVUT CİĞERİ

for 10 persons

1,5 kg. lamb's liver
200 gr. (2 cups) flour
salt
1 table spoon chili powder
1 teaspoon sumac
5 onions medium
1 bunch parsley
thyme
2 cups sunflower oil

PREPARATION
Remove the fine membrane and dice the liver. Rinse well and place in sieve to draine. Sieve the flour and salt, toss the cubed liver in the chili and in the flour, and shake in sieve to remove the excess flour.
Heat the oil to high temperature and add the liver. Fry over a strong heat for 1-2 minutes. Remove with a strainer spoon, place in a serving dish.
Slice the onions finely, rub with salt, rinse and squeeze dry. Mix with sumac, chili powder or paprika and the chopped parsley and serve with the fried liver.

FRIED EGGPLANTS AND PEPPERS WITH TOMATO SAUCE
PATLICAN - BİBER TAVA

for 10 persons

1 kg. eggplants, big
10 green sweet peppers
10 green chili peppers

For the sauce:
8 tomatoes, medium
4 tablespoons olive oil
salt
1 tablespoon sugar
1 teaspoon black pepper
2 table spoons vinegar, 3 cloves garlic

To Fry:
2 cups Sunflower oil

PREPARATION

Peel the aubergines in alternate lengthwise strips (leaving stripes of peel in between), and cut diagonally into 1 cm slices. Sprinkle with plenty of salt and set aside in a sieve for 30 minutes. Peel the tomatoes and grate.

Heat the olive oil in a pan, add the grated tomatoes and simmer over medium heat, stirring frequently until the tomatoes are well cooked. Stir in the salt, sugar and black pepper. Add the crushed garlic and continue cooking. When the sauce has thickened, add the vinegar and set aside.

Wash the aubergines and dry in a cloth or kitchen paper. Heat the sunflower oil and fry the aubergine slices on both sides until golden brown. Drain on kitchen paper. Remove the stalks and seeds from the peppers, and fry whole or divided in half lengthwise. Drain on kitchen paper. Arrange the fried aubergines and peppers on a dish, and pour the hot tomato sauce over. Cover and serve 1 hour later.

This dish can be served with yoghurt on the side, if desired.

Mussels (Pilaki) in Olive Oil
Midye Pilaki

for 10 persons

2 onions, big, chopped
6 table spoons olive oil
2 carrots, small, chopped
100 mussels, cleaned and washed
4 tomatoes, big
1 cup water
5 cloves garlic
1 table spoon sugar
salt, pepper
1/2 bunch parsley, chopped
3 potatoes, medium

PREPARATION

Sauté the onions over medium heat with olive oil for 5 minutes. Add the carrots cut in cubes and saute for 5 more minutes. Finally add the mussels, cubed potatoes, tomatoes, garlic, sugar, pepper and water and cook for 15-20 minutes over medium heat, until the liquid of the vegetables boils away. Serve with lemon slices and parsley on the side.

HORSE BEAN PUREE
FAVA

for 10 persons

500 gr. dried horsebeans
350 gr. fresh horsebeans
8 cups water
1 onion
3 potatoes
1 1/2 cups olive oil, extra
1/2 cup sunflower oil
salt
4 tea spoons sugar
1 pinch dill, minced

PREPARATION

Pick over and wash the dried beans, place in a saucepan with the fresh beans and cold water. Add the chopped onions, and potatoes chopped into cubes, olive oil and sunflower oil. Sprinkle the salt and sugar over. Cover and cook over a medium heat, stirring occasionally with a wodden spoon, until the ingredients are reduced to a puree. Put trough an electric blender. The puree should be of a thick pouring consistency. Pour into a wet mould or dish with raised edges and leave to cool.
Place the fava into a serving dish and decorate with dill to serve.

TARAMA

TARAMA

for 10 persons

1/2 loaf white bread (crumbs)
300 gr. Tarama (a spread made with fish roe)
4 tablespoons lemon juice
3 table spoons water
500 gr. sunflower oil
salt

PREPARATION

Soak the white bread in plenty of water. Take out and press in your hands to leave excess water. Add tarama to the white bread puree. Stir and sieve into a clean bowl. Add the lemon juice, salt and water to the mixture stirring continously. Trickle the sunflower oil in and stir. Garnish with dill lemon juice and olive oil and serve.

BULGUR SALAD
KISIR

<u>for 10 persons</u>

350 gr. bulgur,
1 cup water, hot
1 table spoon red pepper puree
1 table spoon chili flakes
salt
1/2 tea cup lemon juice
3/4 cup olive joil, extra
1 bunch parsley
1 bunch fresh mint
1 bunch spring onions
2 tomatoes, medium
1 crisphead lettuce

PREPARATION

Place the bulgur in a large mixing bowl. Pour over the hot water. Mix and cover. 30 minutes later, add the red pepper puree, tomato puree, chili flakes and salt. Knead thoroughly. Add the lemon juice and the olive oil. Knead again. Add the tomatoes, the chopped parsley, mint and spring onions into the bulgur.

Heap onto a serving dish with the lettuce leaves, or arrange individual portions in each lettuce leaf.

CHICKPEA PUREE
HUMUS

for 10 persons

500 gr. chickpeas
1 teaspoon carbonate
1 cup sesam puree
1/2 tea cup lemon juice
1 tea spoon sugar
3 cloves garlic
salt

PREPARATION

Soak the chikpeas overnight in warm water. Drain the water the next day, add the salt and the carbonate and boil in plenty of water. Blend the cooked chickpsas in to a puree. Clean the garlic cloves and mash them. Add the lemon juice, sesam puree, salt, sugar and garlic to the mashed chickpeas. Transfer the humus to a serving dish, and spread it with the back of a wet metal spoon. Decorate with parslay leaves, lemon juice and olive oil and serve.

SOUPS
ÇORBALAR

Soups have traditional importance and are generally served as the first course. Eaten on every meal including breakfast, they are warm and misty, to help us in cold winter days.

Soups are nourishig, natural and varied in Turkey. Tarhana soup is made of a savoury dough made and dried in summer which is cooked with tomato paste and water. Prepared in advance and cooked months later, tarhana may be the ancestor of modern instant soups.

Spicy and pungent hot yoghurt soup brings the scent of valleys into houses as its Turkish name suggests. Lentil soup and chicken soup are cooked by every housewife. Fish soup prepared in coastal regions adds different tastes to Turkish cuisine. Beef's tribe soup is a help to imbibed stomachs after a long night of drinking rakı; wedding soup made of mutton neck is served on wedding feasts. These two soups are the authentic examples of Turkish soups.

There are four different types of cooking soups: consomes with vermicelli, vegetables, rice and meat like chicken vermicelli; vegetable pastes with butter and flour roux like tomato soup; with yoghurt like green bean soup; cultured with lemon juice and eggs like cultured chicken soup.

The only exception to hot soups is cacık served cool or cold in the summer. Cacık is not a starter but a cooler to be eaten with the main course and pilaf.

TARHANA SOUP WITH MINCED MEAT
TARHANA ÇORBASI

for 10 persons

200 gr. tarhana
2,5 lt. meat stock
2 cups water
4 table spoons butter
salt
250 gr minced meat (sheep, without fat)
1 table spoon paprika (chili pepper)
tomatoes

PREPARATION

Put the meat buillon in a pan and boil. Dissolve tarhana in two cups of cold water for 20 minutes. Add remaining water, stir. Cook over low heat until thickened, stirring constantly. Add salt. Blend paprika and, minced meat in butter, add tomatoes and cook for 2 more minutes. Sprinkle over soup before serving.

WEDDING SOUP
DÜĞÜN ÇORBASI

for 10 persons

1 kg. neck of lamb
15 cups (2,5 lt.) water
1 teaspoon salt
4 tablespoons butter
1 teaspoon chili pepper
for the sauce:
6 tablespoons flour
4 tablespoons yoghurt, thick
2 tablespoons lemon juice
1 egg yolk

PREPARATION

Place the meat in a pan with 13 cups of water and bring to the boil. Skim off the scum, then cover and simmer until the meat is nearly tender. Add the salt and continue cooking until the meat separates easily from the bones. Drain and save the stock. When the meat has cooled, remove the bones and chop finely.

Bring the stock to the boil. Meanwhile mix the flour, yogurt, egg yolk and lemon juice and add 2 cups of water gradually, beating until smooth. Stir gradually into the boiling stock, bring to the boil again and strain.

Add the chopped meat and simmer for a few minutes.

Melt the butter in a pan, stir in the red pepper and pour over the soup to serve.

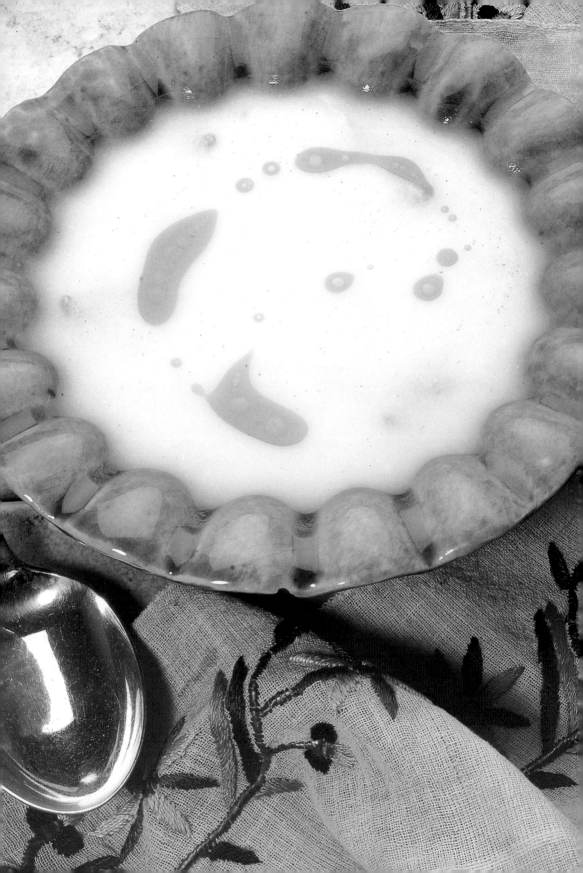

CREAM OF VEGETABLE SOUP
EZME SEBZE ÇORBASI

<u>for 10 persons</u>

2 carrots
3 potatoes
2 onions
2 celery roots
3 table spoons butter
3 table spoons flour
salt
3 lt. meat stock

PREPARATION

Peel the onion and cut into small semi-cireles. Chop the other vegetables into small pieces. Put the butter in a pan and add the vegetables, cook at medium heat for 5 minutes, stirring. Add the flour, stir, add the salt and meat stock and cook for half an hour. When ready, put through a blender and serve with croutons.

EZO GELİN SOUP
EZO GELİN ÇORBASI

for 10 persons

3 cups red lentils
2 onions, medium
2 table spoons tomato paste
2 cups bulgur (boiled and pounded wheat)
45 gr (2 table spoons) butter
2 tea spoons red pepper
2 tea spoons mint
10 cups (2 lt.) meat stock
salt
1 table spoon chili pepper
2 tea spoons thyme

PREPARATION

Chop the onions. Mix the tomato paste with some water in a bowl. Melt the butter in a saucepan and cook the onions until they soften. Add the water (meat stock) and the tomato paste and bring the soup to the boil. Wash the lentils and the boiled and pounded wheat seperately, then sieve and add to the boiling soup. Stir the salt in the soup. Cook the soup until the lentils and the boiled and pounded wheat are tender, stirring continuously.
Serve the soup with chili pepper, and thyme, taste the soup and serve.

LENTIL SOUP
SÜZME MERCİMEK ÇORBASI

for 10 persons

3 cups lentils
2 lt. meat stock
3 onions, medium
100 gr. butter
salt
1 cup (100 gr.) flour

PREPARATION

Soak lentils in cold water and drain. Put one table spoon of butter in a pan and melt. Add the onions chopped into semi-circles and cook at medium heat for 2-3 minutes. Add the flour and stir for 3 more minutes, add the lentils and cook at low heat for 30 minutes.
Remove the soup from the heat and strain, check the salt. Serve with croutons.

CHICKEN VERMICELLI SOUP
ŞEHRİYELİ TAVUK ÇORBASI

<u>for 10 persons</u>

<u>1 chicken (washed)</u>
<u>3 dried onions, peeled</u>
<u>1 tomato peeled and chipped into cubes</u>
<u>1 table spoon vermicelli</u>
<u>1/2 table spoon lemon juice</u>
<u>salt</u>
<u>1 tea spoon pepper</u>
<u>3 liters water</u>
<u>1/2 pinch parsley</u>

PREPARATION

Put the chicken, onions and water into a sauce pan and let boil. Skim off the scum, and cook in slow heat. Take the cooked chicken, put into another pan with cold water, take off the heat and chop the chicken into the size of matches. Strain the chicken sauce, put in the tomato and boil for 5 minutes. Toss in the vermicellis, the chicken and the salt and boil for 5 more minutes, and check the taste. Serve with parsley leaves.

CUCUMBER WITH YOGHURT
CACIK

for 10 persons

5 cucumbers, medium
1 kg. yoghurt, thick
6 cloves garlic
2 cups water
1/2 tea cup olive oil
1/2 pinch dill
salt

PREPARATION

Peel the cucumbers, cut lengthways into 4 and chop into small pieces.
Stir the yoghurt in a deep dish. Mince the garlic cloves with salt and add
to the yoghurt, together with the cucumbers. Stir continuously and add
the water slowly.
Add the olive oil and decorate with dill before seruing.

TRIPE SOUP
TERBİYELİ İŞKEMBE ÇORBASI

<u>for 10 persons</u>

<u>1 kg. veal tripe, cleaned</u>
<u>4 lt. (20 cups) water</u>
<u>1 tablespoon salt</u>
<u>1/2 cup vinegar</u>
<u>2 tablespoons lemon juice</u>
<u>4-5 cloves garlic</u>
<u>3 onions, small</u>
<u>2 tablespoons sunflower oil</u>

for special sauce:
<u>2 egg yolks</u>
<u>3 tablespoons flour</u>
<u>1/2 lemon juice</u>
<u>1.5 cups water</u>

dressing:
<u>4-5 cloves garlic</u>
<u>1/2 cup vinegar</u>

PREPARATION

Wash tripe, cover with cold water and bring to the boil. Pour off water, add 20 cups cold water and onion and return to heat. Add 2 teaspoons salt, vinegar, garlic, onions and sunflower oil. Cover and simmer gently for 2 hours until tender.

Remove onion and discard. Take out the tripe and cut into small strips. Drain the rest of the water, and put 10 glasses of it into a pan with the sliced tripe, and boil. In a deep bowl mix the ingredients for the special sauce and add 1.5 cups of water. Also add a little of the water in which you cooked the tripe. Add this to the boiling soup slowly, stirring constantly. Add the salt, stir and remove from heat. You may serve the mixture of garlic and vinegar seperately with the soup.

FISH SOUP
BALIK ÇORBASI

for 10 persons

1 kg. scorpion fish
500 gr. red gurnard
3 lt. (15 cups) water
3 onions, bip
2 celeries, small with leaves
4 potatoes, small
4 carrots, small
8 black pepper grains
1/2 bunch parsley
6 cloves garlic
2 tablespoons vinegas
1 lemon

PREPARATION

Have the scorpion fish filleted, taking off the skin. Save the head and the fishbone. The red gurnard should also be filleted. Put both the fish fillets and the remaining parts of the fish except for the skins into a big saucepan with 3 lt. of water, and boil with the lid open, until the fish begins to flake itself. Add a peeled onion and boil for 10 more minutes, simmering.

Remove pan from the heat and strain the stock in another saucepan when cold, ramove the fillets and throw the rest of the fish away. Brake the fish into small pieces. Try to remove all the bones, however small. Peel the vegetables, cut into small cubes, put the potatoes and celery into water so that they will not change color. Remove the leaves of the celery and mince them. Wash the parsley and mince. Put the stock to boil, add the carrots, boil for 5 minutes and then add the potatoes and celeries. Boil with the lid closed. Add the minced celery leaves. When the vegetables are cooked, add the chopped fish and the black pepper grains cut into two halves. Boil for 5 more minutes, add the parsley, salt, mashed garlic and vinegar and stir. You may add some lemon juice while having the soup.

YOGHURT AND MINT SOUP
YAYLA ÇORBASI

for 10 persons

1 tea cup washed rice
2 lt. meat stock
salt
1 cup flour
3 tablespoons butter
1 teaspoon dry mint
500 gr. yoghurt
2 egg yolks
1/2 pc. lemon juice
water or milk

PREPARATION

Clean the rice and keep in warm water for 30 minutes. Put the meat stock (2 lt.) and rice into a pan add the lemon juice and salt and cook for 20 minutes in low heat.

Stir the milk and the flour and add to the boiling soup, boil for 10 more minutes. Slowly stir the mixture of yoghurt and egg yolks into the boiling soup. Melt the butter in a pan, add the dry mint. Pour into the soup, cook for 5 more minutes. Serve.

FISH AND SEAFOOD
DENİZ ÜRÜNLERİ

There are many doorless, windowless shops open all-year in Turkey, which sell fish and seafood laid in colourful, round, wooden trays. Turkey is a peninsula having shores on three sides, these seas contain many varieties of fish. Some examples to most common species are mackerel, red mullet, blue fish, sardines, horse mackerel, large bonito, bonito, tuna fish, anchovy, grey mullet, turbot. Lobsters, crabs and oysters are expensive and thus only exist on the tables of the rich. Shrimp, mussel and squid are the other seafoods which are frequently used.

Coastal cities, especially Istanbul and Izmir, use seafood frequently,

whereas the other cities do not use fish in their local cuisine. Istanbul, host of the Ottoman Palace and thereby traditional Turkish cuisine, has been the birth place of a dish called 'uskumru dolması' -mackerel stuffed with nuts, raisins and spices, which is full of creativity.

Fish are generally fried by blending with flour; steamed with a little water; or grilled. People experiencing fish in Turkey think that fish is cooked in only these three ways. However, in Turkish cuisine seafood is also used in soups, pilafs, casseroles, on skewers, stewed.

Among all varieties, there is a special one related to Blacksea people; hamsi-anchovy. Figures in folk dance of this region symbolise fidgeting anchovies. Anchovies are used in many inconceivable ways. They are pickled, grilled, dried and used in soups, böreks, breads, pilafs and desserts.

The most popular seafood is the mussel; dipped in batter and fried served with tarator sauce; stuffed; used in pilaki and pilaf.

SWORDFISH ON SKEWERS
KILIÇ ŞİŞ

10 portions

1800 gr. fillet of sword fish
4 tomatoes, medium
2 sliced lemons
5 green sweet pepper
30 small bay leaves

for the marinade:
1 onion grated
5 bay leaves
2 cloves garlic crushed
1 tea spoon black pepper
1 tea spoon salt
2 table spoons lemon juice
1 cup olive oil
1 table spoon tomato paste

PREPARATION

Take out the bones and skins of the fish. Cut the fish into large cubes of 3 cm.. Slice tomatoes and remove the seeds. Slice the peppers. Put the fish in a bowl, add the marinade ingredients and mix with your hand, leave for 20 minutes. Thread 4 cubes of fish per person onto metal barbecue skewers with slices of tomato, pepper, lemon and bay leaves. Take what is left of the marinade and brush generously over the prepared skewers. Pour any remaining marinade over the top and leave for 5 minutes to improve the taste.
Grill over charcoal or under a hot electric grill, turning frequently, and basting with the marinade.
Garnish with lemon slices, boiled potatoes and serve with salad.

BAKED BONITO
FIRINDA PALAMUT

for 10 persons

3 bonitos, medium size
3 onions, medium
3 tomatoes, medium
6 green chili pepper
1/2 bunch persley
4 bay feaves
salt
2 lemons
1 tea cup olive oil

PREPARATION
Gut the fish and cut into 2 cm. wide circles. Salt lightly and arrange in a baking tin.
Peel and slice the tomatoes, remove the stalks and seeds of the peppers and cut in two. Lay the tomatoes, sliced onions, peppers and chopped parsley over the fish. Place the bay leaves on top and pour over the olive oil. Finally add the slices of peeled lemon. Pour in enough water to sprinkle over the base of the tin to prevent the fish from sticking. Cover with aluminium foil and bake in preheated oven at 180°C until the peppers are tender. Remove the foil and bake until the fish browns slightly.
Place on a dish and serve hot.
P.s. Carrote and celery may be added if desired.

FRIED TURBOT
KALKAN TAVA

10 portions

3 kg. sliced turbots
2 cups flour
2,5 cups sunflower oil

for the marinade:
1 tea spoon black pepper
1/2 tea cup lemon juice
1/2 tea cup olive oil

PREPARATION

Slice the turbots into 3 cm. stripes and put them inside a bowl with black pepper, lemon juice and olive oil.

Dip the marinated turbot slices in flour, and remove the excess flour. Heat the oil in a large deep frying pan and fry both sides of the fish until they reach a golden color. Remove unto several layers of kitchen paper to eliminate excess fat. Serve with lemon slices. You may also cook the slices without marinating them.

POACHED ANCHOVY
HAMSİ BUĞULAMA

10 portions

2 kg. anchovies (hamsi)
4 tomatoes, medium
2 onions
4 sweet green pepper
5 bay leaves
100 gr. butter
2 lemons
1 bunch parsley, chopped
salt
pepper
2 cups water

PREPARATION

Gut the fish, wash and drain. If you have to gut them yourself, put the anchovy in your left hand backwards. Hold the bottom of the head with the thumb and forefinger of your left hand. Hold the head with your right hand and pull slightly foreward and take out the backbone as well. Then wash and drain. Slice the onions. Peel the tomatoes, remove the seeds and slice into small cubes. Slice the peppers after removing handle and seeds. Melt the butter in a pan, add the onions, tomatoes and sweet peppers and cook for 5 minutes, stirring. Add two cups of water and boil. Place part of this material in a baking dish and add the anchovies. Spread the rest of the ingredients over the fish and add the juice of a half lemon. Slice one lemon after peeling and add them to the dish together with the bay leaves. Then spread the salt and the ground black pepper. Cover with aluminum foil and bake in a preheated oven at 160 °C for 15 minutes. After removing from the oven add the sliced parsley leaves and serve hot.

SEA BASS EN PAPILLOTE
KAĞITTA LEVREK

10 portions

1800 gr. nett seabass fillet
2 onions, medium
6 mushrooms, big
4 tomatoes, medium
3 sweet green pepper, medium
10 potatoes, medium
salt
4 bay leaves, 1 cup water
100 gr. butter, 1 lemon juice
1 bunch dill
3 pieces wax paper

PREPARATION

Cut the seabass fillets in 20 equal pieces, put them in a dish and add some salt. Peel the tomatoes, remove the seeds and cut into small cubes. Peel the onions and cut to your liking. Remove stems and seeds of the peppers and slice. Boil the potatoes and cut in each from the middle into 2 pieces. Save some of the butter melt the rest and stir after adding onions, sliced mushrooms, tomatoes and peppers. Add bay leaves, lemon juice and water and cook for 10 minutes with the lid closed on low heat.

Then add these to the fish and cook for another 10 minutes.

Fold the wax paper into two and then four and cut a half heart with scissors. When opened they should become whole hearts. Have 10 such cuttings. Brush butter on each paper, and put 2 slices of fish on one side of the paper, add some of the sauce you prepared and put one slice of potato on top. Add some minced dill. Fold the paper on top of each other, starting from the upper part of the heart. Our aim here is, to prevent the liquid and vapor from leaking. Brush some water on the paper, Put the packages in a boiling dish with liguid oil, and boil for 15-20 minutes in a preheated oven at 170 °C, until the paper is colored.
Serve hot in the paper packeges.

FISH BALLS
BALIK KÖFTESİ

10 portions

2 kg. fish fillet, white
10 spring onions
100 gr. white sesame
3 tea spoons ginger
3 tea spoons curry
salt
3 eggs, beaten
1 table spoon lemon juice
20 ml rakı

to fry:
1 cup flour
4 eggs
500 gr. fine white flour
500 gr. sunflower oil

PREPARATION

Put the fillet fish through a blender. Mix with minced spring onions, sesame, ginger, curry, salt, eggs, lemon juice and rakı with the fish. Mix to a firm paste. Shape the mixture into small balls using both your hands. Coat the balls with flour, beaten eggs and fine white flour and deep fry in hot oil. Serve hot.

SARDINES IN VINE LEAVES
ASMA YAPRAĞINDA SARDALYA

10 portions

50 sardines
50 fresh wine leaves

to marinade:
salt
2 lemon juice
1 tea spoon white pepper grains
1 cup olive oil

PREPARATION

Remove the backbones of the fish but keep the heads and the tails. Scrap the scails and wash them. Mix the marinade ingredients in a bowl. Drain the fish thoroughly and put them in a large bowl, spread the marinade on them and leave. Cut the stems of the vine leaves and soak in hot wates and then in cold water if the leaves are fresh. If they are pickeled keep in warm water for some time to remove the salt.

Put the shiny sides of vine leaves on a clean surface.

Place one sardine on the steam of each leaf. Roll up the leaves and place on a baking tray with stem-side up. The heads and tails of the sardines should not be rolled in the leaves.

Brush the leaves with oil.

Grill stuffed leaves on both sides over medium heat or charcoal about 15 minutes. Garnish with lemon slices. Open vine leaves and sprinkle fish with lemon juice when eating. Serve hot as a main course with a salad.

GREY MULLET IN OLIVE OIL
KEFAL PİLAKİ

10 portions

2 kg. grey mullet with bones
4 onions, medium
4 carrots, medium
10 potatoes, medium, peeled
1 cup sunflower oil
5 bay leaves
4 tomatoes, medium
2 lemons
salt
1 cup water
1/2 pinch parsley
1/2 pinch celery leaves
2 cloves garlic, sliced

PREPARATION

Cut the onions in semi circles. Peel the tomatoes and slice into cubes. Slice the carrots diagonally and the potatoes in slices. Mince the parsley and the celery leaves. Slice one of the lemons and squeeze the juice of the second one. Cut the head and tail of the fish and gut it. Place the fish in a heat resistant serving dish. Heat the oil in a pan and fry the onions pink, add the carrots and potatoes and stir for 3-4 minutes. Add celery leaves, tomatoes, lemon juice and water and cook for 10 minutes. Remove from heat.
Spread the cooked vegetables over the fish and add the sliced lemons and bay leaves. After adding the salt, top the fish with water and cover with wax paper. Bring to a boil and then cook in medium heat. Serve warm.
P.s. you can serve with minced parsley or dill if you so desire.

STUFFED MUSSELS
MİDYE DOLMASI

10 portions

30 mussels with shells
3 onions, medium
1 tea spoon sugar
1/2 cup olive oil
2,5 cups hot water
1 lemon
2 sheets wax paper
salt
pre prepared stuffing for dolma içi (page 136)

PREPARATION

Scrape the mussel shells with an old knife or scrub with a wire brush. Leave to soak in water, while preparing the zeytinyağlı dolma stuffing. Open each shell with a knife taking care not to pull the two sections apart. Cut the hairy beard of the mussel. Wash and and leave to drain. Fill each shell with a tablespoonfull of stuffing, and close. Spread the onions in the bottom of a large saucepan. Wet a sheet of wax paper, squeeze and lay over the onions. Arrange the stuffed mussels on top in neat layers. Add the salt, sugar, hot water and olive oil.
Peel the lemon, cut into slices, and arrange over the mussels. Lay another wet sheet of wax paper over the top, and weigth down with a plate. Cover and bring to boil. Cook over a gentle heat for about 30 minutes until the liquid has evaporated. When the mussels are cooked the shells will open of their own accord, and the mussels themselves will no longer be attached to the inside of the shell.
Without removing the lid set the saucepan aside to cool. Serve with lemon wedges and dill. To give an attractive shine to the shells, lightly brush whith oil.

FRIED MUSSELS
MİDYE TAVA

60 big mussels
2 cups flour

for coating:
1 cup flour
1,5 cups beer

for frying:
1/2 lt. sunflower oil

PREPARATION

Mussels without their shells and their black beards cut, should be washed thoroughly and drained on paper towels. Spread the flour on a tray. Toss the mussels in flour and coat both sides. Mix 1 cup of flour and 1,5 cups of beer into a batter. Toss the flour coated mussels in this mixture and then into deep fried oil. Fry both sides to a golden color. Remove and drain on paper towels. Spread some salt on the fried mussels and serve with tarator sauce on the side.

TARATOR

300 gr. walnuts
5 slices white bread crumbs, wet
4 cloves garlic
2 lemon juice or vinegar
300 gr. yoghurt, creamy
olive oil

PREPARATION

Place the walnut and crushed garlic in a blender and process for 1 minute. Add the lemon juice and the white breadcrumbs. Process for another minute and add the yoghurt. Pour in a bowl when it comes to the consistency of a sauce. If necessary add some cold water. You can serve this sauce with fried mussels.

VEGETABLES AND PULSES
SEBZE YEMEKLERİ VE BAKLİYAT

The mild climate of Turkey is suitable to grow very different kinds of fruits and vegetables which are presented in colorful and cheerful market places arranged neatly in rows together with herbs, pulses and spices.

These market places are so attractive that you can not just pass by without buying an item. Vegetables are never treated as second class. in the Turkish cuisine. They may be sauteed or fried, like sauteed spinach; cooked in olive oil, like green beans in olive oil or cooked with meat, poultry, pastırma or sucuk (both spicy charcuterie) to be served as main course. They are also used lavishly in salads, böreks, mezes and soups. Among all vegetables, eggplants have a special place. They are cooked in nearly fourty different ways. They are fried, stuffed, baked, charcoaled and used in böreks, jams pilafs, kebaps. Most popular examples are; karnıyarık; baked aubergine stuffed with minced meat, tomato, parsley and onion, imam bayıldı; cooked in olive oil stuffed with onion and tomato, salad made of charcoaled aubergine, with a smoky odor and taste. Green vegetables like spinach, chard, purslane are not accessories served with meat as in foreign cuisines, they are cooked with onion and tomato with a little water, served with yoghurt or cooked with a little fat to which eggs may be added if desired.

Besides vegetables, pulses are mainly consumed in winter.In summer fresh and green pulses are widely used. White beans either with pastırma, sucuk or meat is the favorite and served with plentiful of rice pilaf and mixed pickled vegetables and generally onion.

VINE LEAVES WITH MEAT STUFFING
ETLİ YAPRAK SARMA

<u>for 10 persons</u>

<u>500 gr. vine leaves</u>

for the stuffing:
<u>500 gr. minced lamb</u>
<u>5 onions, medium</u>
<u>1 tea spoon salt</u>
<u>3 table spoons rice</u>
<u>1/2 pinch each (150 gr) mint, parsley, dill</u>
<u>1 tea spoon black pepper</u>
<u>1 tomato, big</u>
<u>1 cup cold water</u>

for the sauce:
<u>1 table spoon butter or margarine</u>
<u>1 tea spoon tomato paste</u>
<u>2,5 cups water</u>
<u>1 piece wax paper</u>

PREPARATION

Chop the onions. Peel the tomatoes and dice small. Place the stuffing
mixture in a bowl, add 3/4 cup of water and mix well. Mix and set aside.
Boil the vine leaves for 2 minutes in salted water. Take out the boiled
leaves separatly with a sieve. Divide the leaves into two.
Place a walnut sized lump of stuffing at the base of the leaf, fold the
sides over and roll up. Place the dolmas in a saucepan in layers.
To prepare the sauce, melt the butter in a saucepan. Dice the tomatoes
and add to the melted butter with the tomato paste, salt and stir over the
heat until the tomatoes soften. Add 2,5 cups of water. Bring to the boil

and pour over the dolmas cover the dolmas with wet paper. Place a plate over the dolmas to weight it down. Cover and bring to the boil. Cook over a low heat for about 45 minutes.

Serve with yogurt on the side.

CHARD WITH MEAT STUFFING
ETLİ PAZI DOLMASI

<u>10 portions</u>

4 bunches chards
2 table spoons butter
3 onions
3 cups meat buillons

for the stuffing:
3 table spoons butter
10 (500 gr.) onions
150 gr. rice
1 cup water
minced lamb
salt
1 tea spoon pepper
1/2 bunch dill, chopped
1/2 bunch parsley, chopped
1/2 bunch mint, chopped

PREPARATION

Put the butter in a bowl and melt, then add the onions and stir for 2 minutes. Wash and drain the rice, and add to the onions, boil for one minute then add the water and boil for 4-5 minutes on low heat. Remove the bowl from heat when the rice is rooked. When cooled a little add the minced meat, salt, pepper, parsley, dill and mint and mix all well.
Cut the stems of the chards and boil the leaves in plenty of salted water. Take out the boiled leaves separatly with a sieve. Divide the leaves into two. Place a walnut sized lump of stuffing at the base of the leaf, fold the sides over and roll up. Place the dolmas in a saucepan in layers. Cut the onion into two and place on top of the dolmas. Pour over the water. Add the butter, salt and cover. Bring to the boil and then cook over a low heat for about 45 minutes.

STUFFED CABBAGE
LAHANA DOLMASI

10 portions

2 kg. cabbage
1 table spoon butter
4 onions
salt
meat stock
1 piece tomato

for the stuffing:
2 table spoons butter
500 gr. onions, chopped
150 gr. rice
1 cup water
1 kg. minced lamb
pepper
1/2 pinches each dill, parsley, mint

PREPARATION

Remove the core of cabbage. Separate leaves. Heat salted water in a large saucepan. Bring to boil. Add cabbage leaves. Simmer for 3-4 minutes or until tender. Remove from liquid with a strainer spoon; drain. To prepare the stuffing peel the onions and chop small. Chop the dill finely. Soak the rice in hot water. Rinse and drain. Place in a bowl the minced meat, chopped onions, salt, black pepper, rice, dill and half a cup of water and knead. Divide the cooled cabbage leaves into vine leaves size. Remove any thick veins. Place the stuffing in the center of each leave and fold the edges in over the stuffing and roll. Arrange the dolmas in a large saucepan. Place a plate over the dolmas to weight down. Add 2 cups of hot water, cover and bring to the boil. Then cook for 45-50 minutes over a low heat.

PEPPERS WITH MEAT STUFFING
ETLİ BİBER DOLMASI

10 portions

20 bell peppers, medium
6 tomatoes
1 table spoon butter
3 onions
1 tea spoon sugar
2 cups water, salt

for the stuffing:
3 table spoons butter
500 gr. butter
150 gr. rice
1 cup water
1 kg. minced lamb meat, salt
1 tea spoon pepper
1/2 pinch each dill, parsley, mint

PREPARATION

Remove the stalk of the pepper. Remove the seeds and wash the pepper. To prepare the stuffing, peel and chop the onions. Chop the spring onions, dill and parsley and mint. Wash and drain the rice. Peel the tomatoes and chop small. Remove the stalks and the seeds of the mild chili pepper and slice. Place in a bowl the onion, rice, tomato, pepper, dill, parsley, the minced meat, black pepper, salt and 1 cup of water. Knead and set aside.

Fill the bell peppers with the stuffing. Cut a small piece of tomato as a lid for each dolma. Place the dolmas in a large saucepan.

To prepare the sauce wash and peel the tomatoes and remove the seeds then grate into a bowl. Melt the butter in another saucepan, add the grated tomatoes and sugar. Cook until thickened and pour over the dolmas. Add 3 cups of hot water. Place a plate over the dolmas to weight down. Cover and bring to the boil. Then cook over a medium heat for 45 minutes. Serve with yogurt if desired.

SQUASH (ZUCCHINI) MÜCVER

KABAK MÜCVERİ

<u>10 portions</u>

<u>1 kg. squash</u>
<u>3 onions</u>
<u>2 table spoons butter</u>
<u>1,5 cups flour</u>
<u>1,5 eggs</u>
<u>salt</u>
<u>1 tea spoon pepper</u>
<u>1 pinch dill</u>
<u>3 cups sunflower oil</u>

PREPARATION

Peel and grate the squash and the onions finely. Squeeze to remove the juices. Heat the oil in a friying pan. Add the chopped onions and roast. Add the squash and roast for 2 more minutes then remove the pan from the heat, and pour on a tray. Let cool a little. Then add the eggs, grated white cheese, salt, pepper and dill and knead them.
Fry the sunflower oil in a pan. Take a tablespoon of the mixture at a time and slide into the hot oil. Fry until golden brown on both sides, serve hot.

BRAISED SPINACH ROOTS
ISPANAK KÖKÜ KAVURMASI

10 portions

3 kg. spinach
100 gr. butter
500 gr. onion
salt
2 tea spoons coconut
1 tea spoon pepper
2 cups meat stock
1 tea spoon carbonate

PREPARATION

Cut the roots of the spinach, wash in a plenty of water and rinse well.
Then sieve.
Boil some water, carbonate and salt in a saucepan. Add the spinach roots
and boil for 5 minutes. Pour some cold water over the spinach roots.
Sieve and drain. Chop the spinach. Melt the butter in a saucepan and add
the chopped onions. Braise the onions. Stir in the spinach roots, coconut,
blackpepper and meat stock.
Cook for 15 minutes then serve. You may serve with yoghurt and with
garlic if you desire.

Artichokes With Lamb
Kuzu Etli Enginar

<u>10 portions</u>

1,5 kg. chopped lamb from the shoulder or the legs
150 gr. butter
3 cups hot water
4 onions, medium
10 artichokes, big
salt
1 bunch dill
8 cups wat paper

to soak the artichokes:
2 table spoons water
1 tea spoon flour
salt, 2 lemons

PREPARATION

Rub the artichockes with lemon. Cut off all the hard sections of the leaves. Clean away things that remain in the centre with a small spoon and rub with lemon. Mix water, flour, salt and the juice of one half lemon in a bowl, and add each cleaned artichocke to prevent them from discolouring. Peel the stalks and place those in the water as well.
Melt the butter in a shallow saucepan, add the meat and fry briefly. Cover and cook over a moderate heat until the meat releases its juice, stirring occasionally. Add 1 cup of hot water, cover and bring to the boil. Skim and cook over a low heat until the meat is tender. Peel the onion, cut in half and place in the saucepan with the meat.
Remove the artichokes and their stalks from the bowl and cut each into four. Arrange the artichockes over the meat, placing them the right way up. Sprinkle with salt. Cut out a circle of wax paper to fit inside the saucepan, and place over the artichockes. Cover and bring to the boil. Lower the heat and cook gently, adding more hot water if it begins to dry out. Remove the cover just before serving, otherwise the artichokes will discolour.

To serve, strain off the remaining liquid, and carefully slip the meat and artichokes upside down onto a dish. Pour over the liquid, sprinkle with chopped dill and serve hot.

GREEN BEANS STEW WITH MEAT
ETLİ TAZE FASÜLYE

10 portions

2 kg. green beans
500 gr. tomatoes
4 onions
750 gr. mutton chunks
5 table spoons butter
1 table spoon tomato paste
salt
2 cups water

PREPARATION
Wash the vegetables and snap off ends of beans. Chop the onions finely. Put the onions, meat chunks and butter in a pan and cook for 30 minutes on low heat, lid covered and without adding any water. Add the tomato paste, salt and water and stir. Cut the beans into two pieces and add to the meat. Cook until the beans are tender and serve hot.

WHITE KIDNEY BEAN WITH PASTIRMA
PASTIRMALI KURU FASULYE

10 portions

500 gr. kidney beans
6 table spoons butter
250 gr. pastırma or sucuk
4 onions
1 table spoon tomato paste
salt
8 cups meat stock
500 gr. tomatoes

PREPARATION

Soak the beans in salted water overnight. Wash and boil in plenty of water until they are tender. Strain and place in a saucepan.
Peel the onions and chop finely. Melt the butter in a saucepan. Add the onions and sauté for 3 minutes. Then add the sucuk or pastırma and cook over a low heat until the meat is tender. Add tomato paste and cubed tomatoes and stir. Add the stock, salt and kidney beans and close the lid, cook for 30 minutes, simmering, and serve.
P.S. you may cook the kidney beans, with sucuk, pastırma, meat or on it their own.

Split-Belly Eggplants

Karniyarik

<u>10 portions</u>

10 eggplants, medium, 6 onions, medium
6 cloves garlic, 100 gr. butter
1 kg. minced beef
500 gr. tomatoes, medium
salt
1 table spoon tomato paste
5 cups hot water
1/2 bunch chopped parsley
to fry:
3 cups sunflower oil

PREPARATION

Finely chop the onions and garlic. Peel the tomatoes, and chop small. Chop the parsley. Melt the butter in a saucepan, add the chopped onion and garlic and stir over the heat for a few minutes. Add the minced meat and stir until the juice is released. Add the tomatoes and cook until softened. Finally add the salt and diluted tomato paste. Continue to stir for 5 minutes. Add the hot water and simmer for 5 minutes. Remove from the heat and strain off the liquid into a bowl. Stir the chopped parsley into the minced meat and set aside. Cut off the green sepals from the eggplants, leaving the stalks attached. Slice away little from the pointed ends. Peel the central part, leaving a centimetre of peel at either end. Sprinkle salt over and set aside for 15 minutes. Wash with plenty of water and fry over medium heat until lightly browned. Remove from the fat with a strainer spoon and place in a deep baking tin. With a spoon make a spilt down the eggplant and press out a hollow with the back of the spoon. Fill each eggplant with some of the minced meat mixture. Cut the remaining tomato into 10 slices, remove the seeds and lay one on each eggplant. Pour the liquid from the minced meat over and bake in pre-heated oven at 160°C for about 15 minutes. Serve hot, with rice pilaf.

MIXED VEGETABLE CASSEROLE
YAZ TÜRLÜSÜ

10 portions

750 gr. mutton chunks
500 gr. fresh green beans
500 gr. eggplants
500 gr. fresh okra
500 gr. squash (zucchini)
2 onions
6 tomatoes
6 green chili pepper
6 table spoons butter
salt
2 cups water

PREPARATION

Wash the vegetables. Prepare the green beans and the okra. Peel the squash and the eggplants. Remove the stems and the seeds of the peppers. Cut the green beans, peppers, eggplants and squash into chunks. Chop the onions. Remove the seeds of the tomatoes and cut them into 4 pieces each. Put the meat chunks in a casserole, add butter, onions and peppers. Roast on medium heat until the meat is cooked, add the vegetables and water. Cook until the meat is tender, first on high, then on low heat.

Eggplants Musakka
Patlican Musakka

<u>10 portions</u>

10 eggplants
2 cups sunflower oil
4 onions
250 gr. minced meat
500 gr. tomatoes
salt
250 gr. tomatoes

for decoration:
1 tea spoon pepper
1 pinch chopped parsley
3 cups water
4 table spoons butter

PREPARATION

Cut the stalks of the eggplants and peel. Cut in lengthwise at 1/2 cm thickness. Sprinkle 1 tablespoon of salt over the eggplants and set aside for 30 minutes. Peel the onions and chop finely.
Melt the 4 table spoons of butter in a saucepan and add the onions. Cook for 3 minutes and add the minced meat. Cook for another 5 minutes stirring continously and add tomato, salt and water. Cook for 20 minutes and set aside. Wash the eggplants and drain. Pour some sun flower oil into a saucepan and heat. Add the eggplants and cook. Place the eggplants with a strainer over a kitchen paper to take excess oil. Arrange half of the aubergines into a saucepan and put the minced meat to the center. Place the rest of the aubergines over the minced meat. Arrange the sliced tomatoes over the eggplants. Add the water and bake in a moderate oven for 25-30 minutes.

EGGPLANTS WITH MEAT STUFFING
ETLİ PATLICAN DOLMASI

10 portions

10 egg plants
4 tomatoes
2 table spoons butter
4 onions
1/2 tea spoons flour

for the stuffing:
2 table spoons butter
500 gr. onions
150 gr. rice
1 cup water
750 gr. minced lamb meat
salt
1 tea spoon pepper
1/2 pinch each dill, parsley, mint

PREPARATION

Put 2 table spoons of butter in a pan and melt then add the onions and stir for 2 minutes. Wet the rice and drain and add to the onions. Fry for 1 minute then add a glass of water and boil for 4-5 minutes. Remove the pan from the heat when the rice is cooked. When a little cooled down add the minced meat, salt, pepper, chopped dill, parsley and mint and stir well. Cut the outsides of 2 tomatoes to cover the dolmas. Cut the stems and the other ends of the eggplants and cut into two from their middles. Leave one cm. peels on each side and peel the middle section in stripes, leaving part of the peels on. Hollow out the inside of the eggplants and spraying some salt set aside for 15 minutes. Wash and drain the eggplants, fill them with the stuffing, close with the tomato slices and put these dolmas in a saucepan.

Melt two tablespoons of butter in a pan. Add the chopped onions and flour and cook for 1 minute. Add the meat stock and salt, bring to a boil and pour over the dolmas. Cook over a low heat for 45 minutes.

92

POULTRY DISHES
TAVUK YEMEKLERİ

If you happen to stay overnight in a Turkish village you will wake up at dawntime by the scream of a cock instead of artificial buzzling of alarm clocks. You will see hens, cocks and children running to and fro in the courtyard. Fresh eggs straight from the hen house are eaten at breakfast. Almost every household in villages feeds hens and cocks, guests are served poultry dishes. Amongst poultry, chicken is the one most widely and frequently consumed. However hit of the new year night is the turkey roasted with a stuffing of rice and chestnuts. Goose, quail and duck is also seen rarely in regional cuisines. Harmonious chicken is used in almost every kind of dish. It is used in casserole dishes as in chicken and okra casserole, vegetable casserole; or as fried, grilled. In addition, it is in soups (chicken soup vermicelli), böreks, pilafs and incredibly in desserts. Circassian chicken made of chicken torn in tiny pieces and a walnutty sauce and chicken stuffed with rice and pistachios are the two examples deserving special attention. Mentioing a dessert made of chicken, we shall define the process; chicken breast beaten for a long time is added into a milk pudding and served with cinnamon to be called "tavukgöğsü" meaning breast of chicken.

CIRCASSIAN CHICKEN
ÇERKEZ TAVUĞU

10 portions

1,5 kg. chicken, whole
1 carrot, small
1 potato, small
2 onions, small
10 cups (2 lt) water

for the walnutsauce:
500 gr. walnuts without shells
4 slices white bread, stale
2 tea spoons red pepper
2 cloves garlic
salt
1 1/4 cup chicken stock

PREPARATION

Place the washed chicken, water, the peeled potato, onion and carrot in a large saucepan. Bring to the boil and skim. When the chicken is half cooked add the salt. Cover and continue to cook over a moderate heat until it is tender. When cool, separate the bones and skin and cut the chicken in small pieces. Set the stock apart.

Grind the walnuts finely. Place in a mixing bowl. Soak the stale bread in some of the chicken stock, squeeze and crumble into walnut size. Mix well and add the red pepper, crushed garlic, salt, and knead well.

Place the mixture in a bowl, and beat in 1 cup of warm chicken stock until it is a thick pouring consistency. Mix the pieces of chicken with a few tablespoons of the walnut sauce over, smoothing down with the back of a spoon. Fry the olive oil add the red pepper and stir. Pour over the ingredients and serve.

OKRA WITH CHICKEN
BAMYALI TAVUK

10 portions

750 gr. okra
salt
1/2 cup vinegar
2 onions
2 table spoons butter
500 gr. chicken legs, without bones
4 tomatoes, medium
2 green chili pepper
2 cups meat stock
2 table spoons lemon juice

PREPARATION

Using a small knife, carefully pare the conical ends of the okra without piercing the hollow center. Place in a bowl with hot water, add vinegar and boil for 1-2 minutes. Rinse well and drain. Finely chop the onions. Peel the chicken skin and cut the meat into cubes. Add to the onions and stir over the heat for 5 minutes. Add the tomato and tomato paste, cover and cook over a low heat for 10 minutes. Add 4 cups of hot water, and continue to cook over a medium heat for 25 minutes. Arrange the okra in neat layers in a shallow saucepan. Tip the cooked chicken into a circular space in the saucepan. Add the hot meat stock and lemon juice, and cover with wax paper. Cover with the saucepan lid, and cook over a low heat for approximately 45 minutes.

Chiken With Eggplant Puree
Beğendİlİ Tavuk

<u>10 portions</u>

10 chicken breast and leg
salt
1 tea spoon pepper
4 table spoons butter
100 gr. onion, chopped fine
6 tomatoes
4 bay leaves
100 gr. green chili pepper
2 1/2 cups meat stock

for egg plant puree:
8 (1,5 kg) egg plants
1 lemon
2 cups flour
1 lt. milk
100 gr. butter

PREPARATION

Wash and season chicken pieces with salt and pepper. Sautee chicken pieces in butter 3-4 minutes on medium heat. Add tomatoes, chicken stock, bay leaves, butter, salt and pepper.

Cook covered over low heat until chicken is tender and most of the tomato juice is absorbed. Arrange chicken pieces around a serving platter. Fill the center with eggplant puree. Serve hot..

Eggplant Puree

Pierce the eggplants with a fork, place in a pan over an open flame or on a high gas flame or on charcoal. Cook for half an hour, turning often until the skin blisters on all sides and the eggplant becomes soft. Once the eggplant is cooled down, cut lengthways into two. Scoop out the pulp, squeeze out all the moister and mash with a fork on a wooden board. Place the eggplant pulp into a bowl and add the lemon juice, and set aside.

Place butter in a saucepan, add flour and cook over low heat stirring constantly for 5 minutes. Add boiling milk and continue stirring for 2-3 minutes. Add salt and pepper. Mix eggplants together with this mixture. Mash until it turns into a paste. Serve hot.

STUFFED CHICKEN WITH SPICED PILAF
İÇ PİLAVLI PİLİÇ DOLMASI

10 portions

2 kg. chicken, whole
2 cups rice
150 gr. butter
300 gr. chicken liver
100 gr. pinenuts
50 gr. currant
1/2 tea spoon pepper
1 table spoon tomato paste
1 clove garlic
water

PREPARATION

Wash the chicken. Place the chicken into a saucepan, add 2 cups of water and 2 tea spoons of salt, simmer for 35 minutes. Sieve the chicken stock into a bowl. Take out the chicken bones gently, splitting from the breast towards the neck. Do the same thing for the legs. Thus have a whole chicken without bones.

Wash and rinse the rice under the cold tap until the water runs clear. Melt the butter in a saucepan. Chop the liver in 1 cm cube pieces and stir in the butter with the pinenuts. Simmer 2-3 minutes until the pinenuts turn brown. Add the rice and simmer. Mix the chicken stock with hot water until it becomes 2 2/3 cups and add to the rice. Stir in the currant and salt. Bring to the boil then cook over a low heat for 15-20 minutes. Add the blackpepper and rest for 20 minutes.

Stuff the chicken with 2 tablespoons of pilaf and place it in an oven tray. Mix the tomato paste with some water. Peel the garlic, crush and stir in the tomato paste. Pour over the sauce over the chicken and bake the chicken in a pre-heated medium oven for 20 minutes.

Serve the chicken with the rest of the pilaf.

BOILED CHICKEN WITH VEGETABLES
SEBZELİ PİLİÇ HAŞLAMA

10 portions

10 chicken breast or legs
4 carrots
1/2 leek, lighter parts
3 celeries
1 kg. potatoes
2 lt. chicken stock
salt

PREPARATION

Peel the vegetables. Cut the carrot and the leek into four lengthwise, the potato and the celeries into eight. Chop the vegetables at 2 mm thickness. Wash the chopped vegetables and drain.

Wash the chicken and place in a saucepan. Top with water and bring to the boil. Stir in the vegetables and the salt. Simmer for 25-30 minutes until the vegetables are tender and the chicken is cooked. It is important that the sauce and the vegetables are eaten with the chicken.

CHICKEN ON SKEWERS
Piliç Şiş

10 portions

2 chickens
3 onions
1/2 cup milk
1/2 cup olive oil
salt
1/2 tea spoon pepper
1 tea spoon thyme
6 green chili peppers
25 button onions

PREPARATION

Wash the chicken and take out the bones. Chop the chicken meat into large cubes (approximately 3 cm). Peel the onions, grate and keep the juice. Mix the onion juice with olive oil, milk, salt, black pepper and tyhme. Pour the marinade over the chicken meat and rest for 24 hours. Skin the button onions. Wash the tomatoes and green peppers. Chop the tomatoes into two and slice the green peppers into 3 pieces. Thread 3 cubes of fish onto metal skewers, alternating with slices of tomato, pepper and button onion. Grill over charcoal or under a hot electric grill, turning frequently. Serve with pilaf on the side.

CHICKEN CASSEROLE
PİLİÇ GÜVEÇ

10 portions

10 pieces chicken (breat or legs)
3 onions
250 gr. green beans
100 gr. fresh okra
3 squash (zucchini)
6 green chili pepper
6 tomatoes
salt
1 cup pepper
hot water

PREPARATION

Cut the chicken into serving portions. Sauté chicken pieces in oil for 2-3 minutes and set aside.

Peel the okra. Peel eggplants in stripes and slice thickly. Top, tail and string the beans and cut them into two pieces. Slice the tomatoes. Cut green peppers into strips. Skin the onions. Wash and rinse the vegetablaes. Place eggplant, green bean and okra into the casserole. Season with salt and pepper. Place chicken pieces, tomatoes, and green peppers on top of the vegetables. Pour chicken stock over and add the butter. Garnish with onions and cover.

Put the casserole in pre-heated oven at 180°C and cook for about an hour, until the chicken is tender and vegetables are well cooked.

MEAT DISHES
ET YEMEKLERİ

Turks, who were nomads in Central Asia had a diet consisting mainly of meat, yoghurt and cheese. As hunting is one of the main sources of food, wild animals possessed considerable importance for nomadic Turks. Although Turks are freedom loving and impatient, when it comes to cooking meat they are patient enough to try a variety of methods to improve the taste and texture of meat.

After settling in Anatolia this meat based diet continued and in spite of inflated meat prices today, still continues. Restaurants specialized in cooking meat (kebap houses), specialized in offal dishes (tribe soup shops) and stores selling only meat (kasap) are the silent witnesses of this old meat diet tradition. In feasts, celebrations and weddings, animals are eaten whole rotating on a metal wire hung over charcoal or meat is cut into huge slices and grilled whereas housewives cook meat after cutting into bitable sizes or after mincing. There are many varying meat dishes in the Turkish cuisine. These dishes differ according to cooking methods which are named grills, casseroles, stews, çevirme-rotating over fire, tava-frying, kavurma-cooking with own juice, sahan-in the pan, yahni-cooked with tomato paste, buğulama-steamed, boiled. Meat is flavoured with vegetables, fruits or milk either by marinading or cooking together. The most known meat dishes are döner, kebap, meatballs and stuffed varieties. Traditionally, lamb and mutton are the basic sources of the Turkish diet. However beef has entered Turkish kitchen and seems to be the leading meat source in West Anatolia. Pork never enters a Muslim kitchen although wild boar is often hunted. One interesting reality is that cooking camel meat is permitted by Islam but camels are only seen at touristic towns posing to cameras with a hat on. Additionally hare and deer are cooked rarely in regional cuisines.

Thyme, mint, mild or hot red paprika, cumin, parsley and bay leaf are the most usual companions to meat which is nearly always cooked, marinated or served with onion

Pirzola Servis

İzmir Köfte

GRILLED KÖFTE
IZGARA KÖFTE

<u>10 portions</u>

1,5 kg. minced mutton
1 slice white bread, stale
2 cloves garlic
1/2 tea spoon red pepper
1 tea spoon pepper (black)
1 tea spoon cumin
2 onions, grated
3 table spoons water
1 tea spoon salt

PREPARATION

Remove the crust and soak the stale bread in water for 10 minutes, squeeze well and crumble. Finely chop the parsley. Mix all the ingredients together and knead well. Roll the mixture into ovals. Brush a little oil on both sides.
Grill both sides, 2 minutes each, and serve with charcoaled tomatoes and green peppers.

LAMB ON SKEWERS
ŞİŞ KEBAB

10 portions

2 kg. lamb meat
6 tomatoes
10 green chili pepper
2 onions
1 cup olive oil
1 cup milk
pepper
salt

PREPARATION

Saueeze the onions and put the juice in a bowl and add olive oil, milk and pepper to form a marinade. Cut the lamb meat in chunks and put in the marinade.

Cut the tomatoes into 4 pieces each cut the green peppers in 3 cm. pieces. On each skewer put pieces of meat, tomatoes and peppers and grill both sides. Serve with fried potatoes or pilaf.

BOILED LAMB
KUZU HAŞLAMA

<u>10 portions</u>

<u>2 kg. lamb meat, each</u>
<u>4 piece cut as a portion</u>
<u>4 carrots</u>
<u>6 potatoes</u>
<u>2 celeries</u>
<u>200 gr. shallots</u>
<u>10 cups water</u>
<u>salt</u>
<u>1 pinch parsley, chopped</u>

PREPARATION

Clean the carrots, slice into 4 pieces vertically, 3 cm each. Peel the
tomatoes, cut into 4. Peel the celery and cut into 8 pieces. Place the msat
in a saucepan cover with water and boil over strong heat. When boiled,
remove from heat, drain, wash with cold water and put into another pan.
Add salt and water and cook for 30 minutes over medium heat. Add the
potatoes and other vegetables, cook for 15 more minutes, add the parsley
and serve.
Squash (zucchini) may be added if desired.

SULTAN'S DELIGHT
HÜNKAR BEĞENDİ

10 portions

2 kg. lamb chunks, 4 table spoons butter
3 onions, 1 table spoon tomato paste
1 table spoon flour, salt, 6 tomatoes, 1,5 lt. water
1 tea spoon thyme, 4 cloves garlic
2 bay leaves, 1/2 tea spoon pepper grains
1 pinch parsley stems

for the egg plant puree:
10 eggplants, 1 lemon
4 table spoons butter, 200 gr. milk
500 gr. salt, 1 cup gruyere cheese, grated

PREPARATION

Melt the butter in a saucepan. Add the lamb chunks and roast for 8-10 minutes. Add the sliced onions and the tomato paste, roast for two more minutes and add the flour. Put the thyme, garlic, bay leaves, pepper graines and parsley in a fine muslin and tie tightly. Add this packge to the meat, with salt and water. Add the tomato chunks to the meat and cook for 10-15 minutes over low heat.

Eggplant Puree:

Pierce the eggplants with a fork, place over an open flame or on a high gas flame or on charcoal. Cook for half an hour, turning often until the skin blisters on all sides and the eggplant becomes soft.
Once the eggplant is cooled down, cut lengthways into two. Scoop out the pulp, squeeze out all the moister and mash with a fork on a wooden board. Place the eggplant pulp into a bowl and add the lemon juice, and set aside. Place butter in a saucepan, add flour and cook over low heat stirring constantly for 2-3 minutes. Add boiled milk and continue stirring for 2-3 minutes. Add salt and pepper. Mix eggplants together with this mixture. Add cheese and mash until it turns into a paste for 1 minute. Pour the eggplant puree into a serving dish, make a hollow in the centre and arrange the meat in this hollow with a little of its own juice.

Islim Kebab With Eggplants
Patlicanli İslim Kebabi

10 portions

2 kg. lamb chunks
4 table spoons butter
4 onions, sliced
5 tomatoes
1 table spoon flour
1 tea spoon salt
thyme
2 cloves garlic
1/2 tea spoon pepper grains
1 pinch parsley stems
5 cups water

to wrap the egg plants:
1 kg. eggplants
2 cups sunflower oil
3 tomatoes
5 bell peppers
1 wax paper
10 tooth picks

PREPARATION

Melt the butter in a pan add the meat and roast until the liquid has evaporated. Add the sliced onions and roast further. Chop the tomatoes in chunks, add to the meat, roast for 2 minutes and add the flour. Put the thyme, garlic, pepper grains and parsley stems into a fine muslin and tie tightly. Add this pack to the meat with salt and water. Simmer and cook over low heat for 30 minutes. Throw the herb pack away. Take the cooked meat, put in a bowl and simmer the juice to a pot. Peel the eggplants, cut off their stems and cut into elongated slices 1/2 cm. thick. Put in a bowl and sprinkle salt and rub the eggplants. Wash and drain after 30 minutes. Fry in hot oil.
Cut the tomatoes into two pieces. Remove the stems and the seeds of the

peppers and cut into 4 pieces. Place two eggplant pieces in a coffee cup diagonally, halves overhanging the edges of the cups, put 4 pieces of meat inside, fold the ends of the eggplants over the top. Carefully, turn the bowls upside down into an oven tray. Put a pepper slice and half a tomato overeach package and hold in place with tooth picks. Add the meat juice, top the tray with a wax paper and bake in the oven for 15 minutes. Remove the toothpicks and serve.

LAMB CHOPS WITH TOMATO SAUCE
SAHANDA PİRZOLA

<u>10 portions</u>

40 lamb chops
6 table spoons butter
4 onions, chopped
8 tomatoes
10 green chili pepper
salt
3 cups water
1 tea spoon thyme

PREPARATION

Remove the seeds of the tomatoes and cut into chunks. Melt the butter in a frying pan. Place as many lamb chops as fit in, and fry both sides, then place in a shallow cooking pan. Add the onions and fry and then add the sliced peppers and tomatoes. Add the salt, roast for 2 minutes and add the water. Bring to a boil and add to the lamb chops. Pour the thyme, close the lid, simmer for approximately 30 minutes and serve.

SPRING LAMB STEWED
KUZU KAPAMA

10 portions

2 kg. (10 pieces) springlamb, without bones
salt
3 fresh green chili peppers
6 cups water
5 pinches fresh onions
3 lettuces
2 pinches dill
pepper

PREPARATION

Cover the meat pieces with cold water and boil over high heat. Near boiling, take the meat pieces from the pan and wash with cold water and drain. Put in another pan, add salt, pepper and water. Skin the onions and slice. Clean the lettuces and cut into two halves and wash. Place the drained lettuces and fresh onions over the meat and pour the dill. Bring to a boil, and cook for 45 minutes over low heat.

"LADIES THIGH" CROQUETTES
KADIN BUDU KÖFTE

10 portions

1 kg. minced mutton
4 onions
1 tea cup rice
1 cup water
1 bunch parsley
6 eggs
salt
1 tea spoon pepper
1 cup flour
2 cups sunflower oil

PREPARATION

Drain on paper towels and serve hot.
Skin the onions and chop finely, boil with 2/3 of the minced meat for is minutes with the lid closed, stirring occasionally, until the water evaporates. Wash and drain the rice and boil in a seperate pan with 1/4 cups of water until the rice is tender. Clean and finely chop the parsley. Mix the rice, the cooked and uncooked minced meat, one egg, parsley, salt and pepper thoroughly. Divide the mixture into oval shaped flat balls, and roll in flour. Mix the remaining eggs seperately. Fry the oil, roll the meat balls in the egg mixture, and fry in the hot oil.

ROASTED LAMB
KURBAN KAVURMA

10 portions

2 kg. mutton meat, chunks
3 table spoons butter
6 shallots
salt
1 tea spoon pepper
1 tea spoon thyme

PREPARATION

Melt the butter in a saucepan, add the meat and all the onions and close
the lid. Over medium heat, stir the ingredients until boiled.
When boiled cook for one hour. Add the salt, pepper and thyme. Roast
for 15 more minutes, stirring, and serve.

KEBAB IN PAPILLOTE
KAĞIT KEBABI

10 portions

**4 carrots, 2 celeries, 6 potatoes
6 tomatoes, 4 table spoons butter
1 cup meat stock
1 cup sunflower oil
1 cup peas, canned
4 onions**

**flour
1 table spoon salt, 2 lt. water
2 kg. lamb chunks, 1 tea spoon thyme
4 cloves garlic, 4 bay leaves
1 tea spoon pepper grains, 1 pinch parsley stems, 6 wax papers cut**

PREPARATION

Cut meat, onions, tomatoes and peppers into 1 cm cubes. Combine meat, vegetables and coarsly chopped parsley, blending thoroughly. Sprinkle with salt and peppers. Cut wax paper into half. Place meat and vegetables in the center of sheet. Fold opposite edges over meat overlapping each other. Tuck open ends of wax paper under. Turn upside down. Place in center of other half of the wax paper. Fold in the same manner. Place in a baking pan or in a casserole. Bake in a moderate oven for 90 minutes. Serve hot.

Clean the carrots, peel the tomatoes and the celery. Remove the seeds of the tomatoes. Cut them all in cubes. Put a table spoon of oil into a pan, fry, add the carrots, roast for 2-3 minutes, then add the celery. Stir for 2-3 more minutes and add the meat stock and salt, and cook for 25 minutes. Fry the potatoes in 1 cup of sunflower oil and remove to a plate. Melt the butter in a pan. Add the meat and roast for 8-10 minutes. Add the onions, roast for 2 more minutes, then add the flour. Place the thyme, garlic, bay leaves, pepper grains and parsley stems into a fine muslin and tie tightly, and add this pack to the meat with salt and water. Simmer for 30 minutes and remove the foam with a skimmer. Remove the meat to a tray, throw away the spice pack, keep the juice. Place equal amounts of meat and vegetables on wax paper and fold into packages. Put in an oven tray, roast for 10-15 minutes and serve with the juice.

PRIEST'S YAHNI
PAPAZ YAHNİSİ

10 portions

1,5 kg. veal chunks
6 table spoons butter
10 cloves garlic
1 kg. shallots
3 tomatoes, big
1 table spoon tomato paste
1 tea spoon flour
salt
1 tea spoon ground red pepper
8 cups water
4 bell peppers

PREPARATION

Peel and finely chop the garlic. Peel and wash the shallots. Peel the tomatoes, remove the seeds and chop finely. Remove the stalk and seeds of the pepper and chop finely.

Melt the butter in a saucepan, add the veal and garlic, and cook over a medium heat, stirring occasionaly, until the juice has evaporated. Sprinkle the flour over and stir in. Add the chopped tomatoes, and the tomato paste diluted in a little water, salt and red pepper. Cook for another 10 minutes. Add 8 cups of hot water, cover and bring to the boil. Lower the heat and cook gently for about 15 minutes. Add chopped pepper, and continue to cook until the meat is tender.

VEGETABLES IN OLIVE OIL
ZEYTİNYAĞLILAR

Olives, choosing the Mediterrenean as their natural habitat, are eaten copiously on breakfast and display a very essential role in Turkish kitchen by being squeezed for their oil. Vegetables cooked in olive oil may be the heroes of vegetarian diet with high vitamin and mineral content and charming outlook. These dishes are the sultans, the most respected and cooked dishes, of summer time with appealing odour, taste together with chilliness and lightness.

Turks never utilize vegetables as garnishes or side dishes as they take this as an insult to the vegetables but give them utmost importance by cooking them solely as a nourishing dish. Being cooked in olive oil, they may be eaten with lemon, yoghurt or tomato sauce served warm or chilly. Green beans, eggplants, zucchini, green pepper, artichoke and broad bean are just a few examples to be mentioned out of many.

Creativity in kitchen finds its meaning in stuffed vegetables in olive oil and in stuffed vine leaves. Combining vine leaves,currants, rice, pinenuts, cinnamon, dill, mint and olive oil results in a mouthwatering dish which is the favorite of many people.

Olive oil is used lavishly in cooking vegetables with a little water; in salads, in brekfasts to dip toasted bread.

If you want to meet the real characters of vegetables, to meet modest zucchini, friendly green bean, fiery eggplant and tickling broad bean, try cooking them in olive oil; you'll see the difference

ARTICHOKES IN OLIVE OIL
ZEYTİNYAĞLI ENGİNAR

10 Portions

**10 artichokes
3 carrots
4 potatoes
30 shallots
2 tablespoons flour
1 tablespoon sugar
2 tablespoons lemon juice
10 cups lemon juice
water
5 tablespoons peas, boiled
1 pinch dill
1 cup olive oil
1 wax paper**

PREPARATION

Clean the artichokes with their stalks. Peel the carrots and potatoes and chop fine. Skin the onions.
Put the onions side by side into a sauce pan, with the carrots, potatoes, and onions on top of then. Add the olive oil. Mix the salt, lemon juice, flour and sugar in a seperate bowl and add to the artichokes add the water. Cover the artichokes with wax paper and put a plate above the paper for its weight, bring to a boil, then turn down the heat and boil for 45 minutes over low heat.
When cool add the cooked peas and dill and serve.

Horse Beans in Olive Oil
Zeytinyağli Taze Bakla

10 portions

1.5 kg fresh horse beans
2 onions, medium
2 cups water with flour and lemon
1 cup olive oil
2,5 table spoons sugar
1/4 lemon juice
1/2 bunch dill
500 gr. yoghurt

to wet the horsebeans:
Plenty of water
1 table spoon flour
1/2 lemon juice

PREPARATION

Cut off both edges of the horse beans, rub with plenty of salt, keepin a
big bowl for 10 minutes. Wash under running water and keep soaked for
5 minutes. Remove horse beans from water and string them with a knife,
and put them into a bowl with water, flour and lemon.

Rub the onions with salt after you chop them. Set aside half a cup of
water with flour and lemon. Put a little of the onions into a medium sized
saucepan. Add the horse beans one by one, and continue with a layer of
horse beans and a layer of onions until all the beans are in the pan. Add
the half cup of water with flour and lemon, and the olive oil to the beans
and onions. Sprinkle the sugar, add the water and put a plate on top of
the beans close the lid and cook over high heat first, and low heat later,
for about half an hour until the horse beans are soft. Add the lemon juice
10 minutes before you remove the pan from the heat. Let cool before you
remove the lid. Remove the water. Turn upside down and add the water.
Add dill and serve with yoghurt.

VINE LEAVES WITH RICE STUFFING
ZEYTİNYAĞLI YAPRAK SARMASI

10 portions

1 kg. vine leaves, 2 lemons
1 cup water, 2 teaspoons sugar
2 tablespoons olive oil
salt

for the stuffing:, 1/2 teaspoon rice
3 cups olive oil, 1,5 pinenuts
1/2 cup onions, chopped
500 gr. sugar
1 tablespoon allspice
1/2 cup currants
3 cups water, hot
3 cups parsley, dill, mint
1 pinch each finely chapped

PREPARATION

Wash and remove stems of vine leaves. Reserve stems. Heat 10 cups of water and lemon juice in a large saucepan. Bring to boil. Add vine leaves. Simmer for 4-5 minutes or until tender. Remove from liquid; drain. Complete volume of liquid to 2 1/4 cups. Set aside. Combine finely chopped onions and pinenuts in a saucepan. Add oil. Saute covered for until onions are tender, strirring occasinally. Stir in rinsed and drained rice; mix well. Saute for 4-5 minutes, stirring again. Add the sugar, allspice, currants and the boiling water. Cover and simmer for 10-15 minutes; drain. Remove from heat. Stir in finely chopped herbs. S_ason with spices. Spread some vine leaves, on bottom of a saucepan. Put one tablespoon of the stuffing in each leaf and cover and wrap. Arrange wrapped vine leaves in a saucepan. Heat remaining reserved liquid. Add to wrapped vegetables. Cover and simmer for 50 minutes or until rice is tender. Remove from heat; cool. Garnish with lemon slices. Serve cold.

HORSE BEANS IN OLIVE OIL
ZEYTİNYAĞLI İÇ BAKLA

<u>10 portions</u>

1 kg. horse beans
4 onions
1 cup olive oil
5 teaspoons sugar
salt
3 pieces dill stalks
5 cups water
1 wax paper

PREPARATION

Shell the horse loeans and peel off the skin. Place the horse beans, sliced and peeled onions, the sugar, the olive oil, salt, dill stalkes and water in a saucepan and bring to the boil over a medium heat. Lower the heat and cook for approximately half on hour until the beans are tender. Without removing the lid, set the saucepan aside to cool. Remove the onions and the dill stalks before serving.
Decorate with dill leaves to serve.

ARTICHOKES WITH HORSE BEANS
ZEYTİNYAĞLI İÇ BAKLALI ENGİNAR

10 portions

10 artichokes, 3 onions
1/2 cup lemon juice
1 cup olive oil, salt
6 tea spoons sugar
7 tea spoons flour
1 wax paper
horse beans
2 lemons
2 table spoons flour
10 cups water

PREPARATION

Clean the outer leaves of the artichokes. Cut off the stalks and pare. With a small sharp knife slice away the purple choke horizontally. Pare away the leaves and hard sections until the white heart is left. Rub the artichoke hearts with lemon juice mixed with a little salt so that they do not discolour.

Toss the prepared artichokes into the water mixed with lemon juice and flour. Put 10 cups of water into a large saucepan, add the artichokes, pared stalks, peeled whole onions and other ingredients.

Cover with a round sheet of wax paper and weight down with a plate. Cover and bring to the boil over high heat, then cook over a gentle heat for about 45 minutes. Remove from the heat and set aside to cool without removing the saucepan lid.

Shell the horse beans and peel off the skin. Place the broad beans, whole peeled onions, dill stalks, and other ingredients in a saucepan and bring to the boil over a medium heat. Lower the heat and cook until the beans are tender. Remove from heat and leave to cool. When cool, place the artichokes on a serving dish and fill the centres with the beans.

Pour the juice in wich the artichokes cooked over, and decorate with springs of dill.

Rice Stuffing For Zeytinyağli Dolma

Zeytinyağli Dolma İçi

10 portions

3 cups rice
1,5 cups olive oil
1/2 cup pinenuts
500 gr. onions, finely chopped
2 tea spoons sugar
1 tea spoon allspice
1/2 cup currants
3 cups water, hot
1 pinch parsley, finely chopped
1 pinch dill finely chopped
1 pinch mint finely chopped
salt

PREPARATION

Soak the rice in hot water for 30 minutes, then rinse throughly until the water runs clear. Drain.

Soak the currants in warm water until they swell up. Heat the olive oil in a saucepan, add the pine kernels and brown lightly over a medium heat. Add the finely chopped onions and cook until coloured. Add the rice and stir over the heat for 4-5 minutes.

Add the drained currants, salt, remaining spices and stir into the rice. Add the hot water, bring to the boil and cook over a low heat for about 15 minutes. When the water has evaporated, and the rice gets too tender tip onto a large plate to cool. Chop the mint, parsley, and dill finely and stir into the cooled stuffing.

STUFFED EGGPLANT WITH OLIVE OIL
ZEYTİNYAĞLI PATLICAN DOLMASI

10 portions

10 eggplants
1 tablespoon olive oil
salt
2 teaspoons sugar
1 lemon
2 cups water

for the stuffing:
2 cups rice
1 cup olive oil
1/2 cup pinenuts
500 gr. onions, chopped
1 tea spoon sugar
1 tea spoon allspice
1/2 cup currants
2 cups water, hot
pinch each parsley, dill, mint, chopped

PREPARATION

Cut stem sides of eggplants. Cut into half crosswise. Scoop out pulp completely until 4-5 mm thick shells formed. Pierce with tip of a paring knife. Set aside. To prepare filling, combine finely chopped onions and pinenuts in a saucepan. Add oil. Saute covered for 20 minutes or until onions are tender, stirring occasionally. Stir in rinsed and drained rice; mix well. Saute for 4-5 minutes, stirring again. Add minced tomatoes reserving one, salt, sugar and hot water; stir. Sprimkle currants over.
Cover and simmer for 100-115 minutes; drain. Remove from heat. Let stand covered for 10 minutes. Stir in finely chopped herbs. Season with spices, sprinkle with lemon juice. Fill eggplant shells with filling. Cover open ends with tomato wedges pushing in slightly. Arrange in a shallow saucepan. Add hot water. Sprinkle with salt. Cover and simmer for 50 minutes or until rice is tender. Remove from heat; cool. Serve cold.

PEPPERS WITH RICE STUFFING
ZEYTİNYAĞLI BİBER DOLMASI

10 portions

20 bell peppers
4 tomatoes
salt
1/2 tea spoons sugar
1 cup olive oil

for the stuffing:
2 cups rice
1 cup olive oil
1/2 cup pinenuts
500 gr. onions, chopped
1 tea spoon sugar
1 tea spoon allspice
1/2 cup currants
2 cups water, hot
1 pinch each parsley, dill, mint, chopped

PREPARATION

Remove stems and seeds of peppers. Pierce on bottoms with tip of a paring knife. Set aside. Combine finely chopped onions and pinenuts in a saucepan. Add oil. Saute covered for 20 minutes or until onions are tender, stirring occasionally. Stir in rinsed and drained rice; mix well. Saute for 4-5 minutes, stirring again. Add minced tomatoes, reserving one, salt, sugar allspice and hot water; stir. Sprimkle currants over. Cover and simmer for 15 minutes; drain. Remove from heat. Let stand covered for 10 minutes. Stir in finely chopped herbs. Season with spices, sprinkle with lemon juice. Toss slightly. Fill peppers with filling. Cut reserved tomato into 12 wedges. Cover open ends of peppers with tomato wedges pushing in slightly. Arrange in a shallow saucepan. Add hot water sugar and oil. Sprinkle with salt. Cover and simmer for 45 minutes or until rice is tender. Remove from heat; cool. Serve cool.

RED BEANS WITH OLIVE OIL
ZEYTİNYAĞLI BARBUNYA PİLAKİ

10 portions

500 gr. red beans
3 onions, chapped
4 cloves garlic
1 cup olive oil
2 carrots
2 celeries
3 potatoes
3 tomatoes
salt
4 cups water
1 tea spoon sugar

PREPARATION

Wet the beans and keep in water overnight. Shell the beans, wash and bring to the boil in 6 cups of water. Simmer until partially tender and drain. Peec the onions and garlic and leave whole. Peel the tomatoes, remove the seeds and dice small. Place the tomatoes, whole onions and olive oil into a saucepan and cook over a medium heat until the tomatoes have softened, stirring occasionally. Add 4 cups of hot water, salt sugar, the whole garlic cloves, the vegetables and cooked beans, and stir. Cover and cook until the beans are tender, and only the oil and very little liquid remains. A little more hot water may be added during the cooking process if necessary. Set aside the saucepan to cool with the lid on. Remove the whole onions to serve, and arrange parsley chops on top of the beans.

SWONING IMAM
İMAM BAYILDI

10 portions

10 eggplants, medium
6 onions, medium
6 tomatoes, big
1 cup olive oil
1 table spoon sugar
6 cloves garlic
1 bunch parsley
1 lemon, squeezed
2 cups water

to put the eggplants in:
plenty of water
1 table spoon salt

PREPARATION
Cut off the stems of the eggplants and peel in strips.
Saute eggplants in salad oil until golden brown. Split open eggplants lenghtways leaving both ends uncut. Place them side by side in a single layer open sides up in a shallow and large saucepan. Set aside.
Saute onions in 1/2 cup oil until they are soft and golden brown. Add tomatoes, garlic, parsley and salt. Simmer for 15 minutes. Remove from heat. Stuff the eggplants with this mixture.
Add 1/2 cup olive oil, sugar, salt and water. Cover and cook over medium heat for about an hour until the eggplants are tender. Transfer gently to a serving platter. Serve cold.

GREEN BEANS IN OLIVE OIL
ZEYTİNYAĞLI TAZE FASÜLYE

10 portions

1,5 kg. green beans
1 cup olive oil
3 tomatoes, big
3 onions, big
3 cups water
salt
2 teaspoons sugar
wax paper

PREPARATION

Remove the tops, bottoms and string the beans, then wash. Peel the tomatoes, remove the seeds and chop. Melt the oil in a medium size frying pan and fry the tomatoes. Stir frequently to mash the tomatoes. Arrange the green beans in a medium sized sauce pan. Place the skinned whole onions in the middle of the pan. Skimmer the tomate and oil and add on top. Add the salt, sugar and water and top with wet wax paper. Put a plate above the paper. Close the lid, bring to a boil and simmer for 1 hour. Serve cold.

BRAISED LEEKS
ZEYTİNYAĞLI PIRASA

<u>10 portions</u>

2 kg. leeks
2 onions, medium
2 carrots, medium
2 tomatoes, medium
1 cup olive oil
2 table spoons rice
2 cups warm water
salt
2 tea spoons sugar
1 pc. lemon, squeezed

PREPARATION

To prepare the leeks cut off the base and coarse ends of the leaves, and discard one or two layers of the outer leaves. Wash and cut the leeks into 3-4 cm lengths. Peel the carrots and slice thinly. Peel the tomatoes, cut in half and remove the seeds. Wash and drain the rice. Place the carrots, leeks, whole peeled onions and tomatoes into a saucepan, add the olive oil and 1/4 cup of warm water and cook over a medium heat for 10 minutes. Add 1 3/4 cups of warm water, salt and sugar, and cover. Continue to cook over a medium heat, shaking lightly the pan occasionally so that the leeks do not stick to the base of the pan. When the leeks are slightly soft, sprikle the rice over, cover and cook until only the oil and a little juice remains. Occassionally check that it is not scorching. When the rice is tender, remove from heat and set aside to cool without removing the lid. Remove the whole onion before placing on a serving dish. Serve with wedges of lemon or lemon juice to sprinkle over.

CELERIES IN OLIVE OIL
ZEYTİNYAĞLI KEREVİZ

10 portions

6 celeries, medium
2 lemons, squeezed
15 shallots
3 carrots, medium
3 potatoes, medium
4 table spoons peas
1 cup olive oil
salt
1 tea spoon sugar
1 tea spoon flour
3,5 cups hot water
1 bunch dill
1 wat paper

PREPARATION

Fill a large bowl with water and stir in the juice of half a lemon. Cut away the stalks and base of the celeriacs and peel thickly. Place in the bowl of water to prevent discolouring. Then divide in half and scoop out a shallow hollow. Straighten the edges with a knife. Replace in the water immediately. Dice the carrots and potatoes. Boil the peas until tender. Drain the celeries and arrange in the saucepan. Add the carrots, potatoes, shallots, olive oil, water, salt and sugar cover with wat paper. Weight down with a plate which fits inside, cover and bring to the boil over a high heat. Continue to cook over a low heat. When the vegetables are nearly tender mix the flour and lemon juice with a litlle water and lifting up the wax paper pour over the celeries. Add the peas and shake the saucepan gently. Replace the wax paper and cook for a further 5 minutes. Remove from the heat and set aside to cool with the lid on. Place the celery halves on a serving dish and fill with the other vegetables. Garnish with a little dill.

Olive Oil Pilaf With Eggplants
Zeytinyağlı Patlicanli Pİlav

10 portions

3 1/4 cups rice, large round-grained
8 eggplants, long thin
7 onions, medium
3/4 cup olive oil
5 chili peppers, mild
2 teaspoons salt
2 teaspoons sugar
2 tomatoes

PREPARATION

Cut off the stalks and skin the eggplants in alternate lengthwise strips partially. Cut into four lenghtwise and then into small cubes. Pour in salted water to remove any bitter juice. Pick over the rice, place in a bowl. Cover with hot water, and add 1 tablespoon of salt. Stand for 10 minutes, then wash in cold water and drain. Remove the aubergines from the water, and dry with a kitchen paper. Rub in a teaspoonful of salt and sugar. Fry in hot oil until golden brown. Drain on kitchen paper. Heat the olive oil in medium sized saucepan and gently cook the chopped onions. Add the peeled and diced tomatoes to the onions. Stir over the heat until the juice has evaporated. Add 3 3/4 cups of water, 1 teaspoon each of salt, sugar and allspice. Bring to the boil and add the rice. Stir, cover and bring to the boil again over a high heat. Lower the heat and cook gently until the rice has absorbed the liquid. Finally chop the dill and mint and sprinkle over the rice. Lay the eggplants over the top. Cover and cook over a very low heat for 5 minutes. Remove from the heat and stand covered for 15-20 minutes. Stir the pilaf carefully with a wooden spoon without breaking the rice. Cover and stand for another few minutes then serve hot or cold if desired.

BÖREKS AND PASTRIES
BÖREKLER VE HAMUR İŞLERİ

Flour and everything made of flour is sacred in Turkey. It is a sin to throw bread into waste and if it falls down, it is kissed and picked up. Turkish people are seldom satiated without bread. Shortly, a table without bread is a garden without flower, for the Turkish people. Flour symbolises fertility to Anatolian people and brings fertility to tables by means of varieties of böreks, and pastries.

A pastry is kneaded from water, flour and salt, then rolled into thin sheets called yufka, which is the basic ingredient in a börek. By adding vinegar, olive oil, eggs, milk, yoghurt or butter, different kinds of pastries may be kneaded to combine with fillings of minced meat, white cheese, spinach, poultry, fish and other vegetables which is then called a börek.

Böreks are classified according to cooking-folding method, type of dough and filling. Potato arm börek is folded in a shape of long cylinder and placed in tray a little twisted and baked; cigarette börek is in shape of a cigarette and fried; zucchini börek is made by placing whole yufkas onto tray, spreading grated zucchini in between and baking.

The most popular example is the water börek. Rather coarse yufkas are boiled in salty water and laid on a tray with fillings of white cheese, spinach or minced meat then baked in the oven after being sprinkled with considerable butter.

Another example is mantı which needs skill and patience, made best at Kayseri. Mantı resembles Italian ravioli but the filling is necessarily onion and minced meat, not vegeables. Mantı is eaten as main dish and served with a helping of garlic yoghurt and red pepper sauce.

If you come to Istanbul and see gulls eating simit-sesam seed pastry, thrown by passengers of Bosphorus steamer, do not be surprised. Pastry addiction is reflected to animals.

KEBAB IN PASTRY
TALAŞ KEBABI

20 portions

for the puffpastry:
900 gr. flour
1 egg
2 tablespoons salt
1 tablespoon vinegar
1 tablespoon butter
1 1/4 cups water
530 gr. margarine
To roll out the pastry:
1 cup flour

for the filling:
1 kg. mutton, shoulder or leg
5 onions, medium
3 table spoons butter
salt
1 table spoon tomato paste
3 cups water
1 table spoon sugar
1 tea spoon mint
for bruhing the pastry:
1 egg yolk

Preparing the pastry:
Sieve the flour onto a board, make a hollow in the centre and pour in the beaten eggs, salt, vinegar, butter and 2 tablespoons of margarine. Mix these with the hands, and gradually mix in the flour. Slowly add the water, kneading to a soft, springy dough. Cover with a damp cloth and set aside for 15 minutes. Knead again and set aside for 5 minutes. Roll out an oval shape on a floured board. Place 500 g margarine in a block in the centre, and fold the corners over to meet in the centre. Roll out, spreading the margarine over the pastry. Brushing away excess flour fold the two short ends into the centre, and fold out to 5 mm in thickness.

Fold the opposite edges to meet in the centre again, and roll out lightly. Wrap the pastry in cling foil and then in a damp cloth and refrigerate for 2 hours. Then sprinkle flour over and roll out to a rectangle. Fold two opposite edges into the centre, roll out again, then wrap up in the same way and place in the refrigerator again for another hour. Place on a floured board and flour. Roll out to rectangle, fold in the same way again, then wrap up and put away in the refrigerator until needed.

Preparing the filling

Remove any sinews from the meat, and cut into very thin strips, then into 4 cm lenghts. Cut the onions into four and slice finely. Melt the butter in a saucepan, and gently fry the onions until tender. Add the salt and the meat, cover and cook over a low heat, stirring occasionally. Cook until the juice evaporates. Stir in the tomatto paste, then add the water and sugar, lower the heat and cook approximately 1- 1 1/2 hours. When the meat is tender, drain off any liquidd into a bowl and set aside. Place the meat into a shallow dish, sprinkle mint on top and leave to cool. Roll out the pastry on a floured board into a rectangle 1 cm thick. Cut into 10 x 10 cm squares. Place a little of the cooked meat into the centre of each, and fold over the edges to form a neat package. Arrange in a baking tray, folded edges downwards. Beat the egg yolk and brush over. Bake in a pre-heated oven aat 160°C for about 45 minutes, until the böreks have puffed up and are golden brown. Heat up the gravy and either pour over each or serve separately.

PUFF BÖREK
PUF BÖREĞİ

10 portions

for the pastry:
1 kg. flour, 4 tablespoons margarine, 2 eggs, salt

for the filling:
3 tablespoons margarine, 5 onions, 500 gr. minced mutton
pepper, salt, 1 pinch parsley, chopped

to fry:
5 cups oil

PREPARATION

Sieve the flour onto a board, make a holllow in the centre and break the egg insidee, add the salt, butter, 50 g of the margarine and vinegar, and gradually mix in the flour, working outwards. Add the water slowly, kneading until you have a soft, springy dough. Cover with a damp cloth and set asidee for 10 minutes. Form a long thin roll, divide into pieces 5 cm in length and roll into balls. Flour the board and roll out each piece to the size of a plate with an ordinary rolling pin, then using a long slender Turkish rolling pin roll out to 30 cm in diametre. Melt the remaining 100g of margarine, brush over each sheet of pastry and stack one on top of the other. Do not grease last sheet. Place in a floured baking tray, cover with a cloth and refrigerate for about 1 hour. Mix the onions and meat. Put the stack of pastry sheets onto a floured board, and flouring liberally, roll out all that once until you have a very thin pastry, using a slender rolling pin. Starting 4 cm away from the lower edge of the pastry place teaspoonfuls of the filling at regular intervals in a line. Brush the area between them with water, then fold the lower edge of the pastry over the top and using a knife or pastry cutter cut out around each lump of filling to form moon-shaped pastries. Repeat until finished. Heat 4 cups of sunflower oil in a saucepan and fry the pastries, stirring occasinally with a strainer spoon until they have swelled up and are golden brown all over. Remove onto kitchen paper to drain off excess fat and serve hot.

BÖREK IN A TRAY
TEPSİ BÖREĞİ

10 portions

5 sheets yufka
2 cups milk
4 eggs
8 table spoons (100 gr.) butter
400 gr. white cheese
1 bunch parsley
1/2 teaspoon pepper

PREPARATION

Soak the white cheese in cold water for an hour or so to remove excess salt. Crumble and mix with the finely chopped parsley. Melt the butter and use a little to grease a large circular baking tray with raised edges. Beat the remaining butter, milk and eggs together. Lay one yufka in the baking tin with the edges overhanging the sides equally. Sprinkle a little of the egg mixture over. Divide the second yufka into large pieces, spread over the first and sprinkle with some grated white cheese and egg mixture. Spread the whole third yufka over and sprinkle with a little of the grated white cheese and all the filling. Sprinkle plenty of the egg mixture over. Divide the fouth and fifth into large sections, and lay over the top, sprinkling with more grated cheese and egg mixture. Brush the folded over edges with the remainder of the egg mixture, making sure that it does not run down inside the tray (otherwise the börek will stick to the tray). Bake for approximately 45 minutes in a pre-heated oven at 160°C until golden brown all over. Sprinkle cold water over the top as soon as you remove it from the oven, and cover with a damp cloth. Set aside for a few minutes. Cut into squares 10cm x 10cm and serve hot.

STUFFED DUMPLINGS WITH YOGHURT
MANTI

10 portions

For the pastry :
6 cups flour
salt
6 tablespoons oil
2 eggs
1 cup water

For the filling:
500 gr. minced mutton
salt
2 teaspoons pepper
3 onions

For the sauce:
200 gr. (3 table spoons) butter
5 cloves garlic
4 tomatoes
salt
1 tea spoon red pepper chilli
1 tea spoon mint
To boil the mantı:
15 cups water
salt
To garnish:
1,5 kg. yoghurt
3 cloves garlic

PREPARATION

Place the flour in a bowl, make a hollow in the centre, and place the salt, oil, egg and water in the hollow. Mix the liquid ingredients first, then gradually incorporate the flour. Knead to a fairy stiff paste. Cover with a damp cloth and set aside for 30 minutes. Divide into two and replace one under the damp cloth. Flour the board, and roll out one of the pieces of pastry to 3 mm in thickness with a long slender rolling pin. Cut into long strips 3 cm wide, and then cut into squares.

To prepare the stuffing, grate the onion finely. Add all the other ingredients and mix thoroughly. Place a tiny amount of the stuffing onto each square of pastry, and gathering the opposite corners together in either hand bring towards the centre and press together to form little bundles. Arrange without touching on a floured surface or tray. Bring the water and salt to the boil, and toss the pastry bundles in one by one, stirring occasionally to prevent them from sticking. Simmer for 15 minutes, until they rise to the surface. Cook for a few more minutes then remove from the heat. Remove with a strainer spoon and place in a serving bowl. To prepare the tomato sauce, melt the butter in a frying pan. Dilute the tomato paste in 4 tablespoons of the liquid in which the mantı were boiled and add. If using fresh tomatoes, peel, remove the seeds and grate. Add the salt and cook over the heat until softened. Just before removing from the heat add the chili flakes and dried mint, stir and serve hot in a separate bowl. Crush the garlic and beat into the yoghurt with salt to taste. Serve in a separate bowl. Serve the mantı in soup plates, spooning the tomato sauce and yogurt over the top.

BÖREK ROLLS
SİGARA BÖREĞİ

10 portions

5 sheets yufka
300 gr. white cheese
3 egg yolks
1 pinch parsley, chopped
2 cups sunflower oil

PREPARATION
Soak the white cheese in cold water to remove the excess salt and mash with the egg yolk. Mix in the chopped parsley. Divide the yufka into 8 equal triangles. Place a teaspoonfull of the filling at the base of each triangle and roll up like a cigarette. Wet the pointed end and stick down. Fry the böreks in hot oil until golden brown all over. Serve hot.

PILAFS
PİLAVLAR

Rice has spread out of China to other cultures, and to the Turkish culture. Custom was to eat pilaf just before the dessert to clean the palate, accompanied by hoşaf-compote of dried fruits, by the Ottomans, whereas it turned out to be eaten as a side dish served with meat or vegetable dishes or pulses nowadays.

Pilafs have possessed an essential part in the kitchens of the Palace and the populace, possible to be eaten both at lunch and at dinner. Rice pilaf with chicken and chick pea is so common that it is sold by street vendors. Schools present pilaf to graduates at commemoration days which are named "pilaf days". Turkish cuisine gives the same importance to pilaf as Western cuisines give to potatoes.

The basic ingredient in pilafs are either rice, bulgur (boiled and cracked wheat) or vermicelli. There are varieties of pilafs cooked by adding onion, tomato, vegetables, nuts, herbs, poultry, or meat or combinations of these but generally cooked plain, namely with butter, water and salt.

Rice pilaf is the most common variety. Cooking this pilaf suitably (a good pilaf is white, unsticky, scenty and odorful) is a measure of ability in cooking for the housewives. After pilaf is simmered, it is covered with a cotton cloth to absorb excess humidity. Pilafs are preferably made of long grain rice and shorter types reserved to be used in soups, stuffings and meatballs. Rural areas and Southeastern Anatolia prefer bulgur as it is easier to obtain and cheaper. Bulgur pilaf is cooked with onions and tomatoes and is eaten with yoghurt.

PLAIN PILAF
TEREYAĞLI PİLAV

6 portions

2 cups rice, large round-grained
100 g butter
1/2 teaspoon salt
1 1/2 teaspoons sugar
2 1/2 cups water, meat stock or chicken stock

PREPARATION

Pick over the rice, place in a bowl with 1 tablespoon salt and cover with hot water and stand for 30 minutes. Drain and rinse under the cold water. Drain and set aside. Melt the butter in a medium saucepan and add the rice. Stir over medium heat until the rice grains stop sticking to the wooden spoon. Add the salt, sugar and boiling water or stock, stir once, and cover. Cook over a low heat for about 15 minutes or until the liquid has evaporated and steam holes appear in the surface. Remove from the heat and seat aside without removing the lid for 10 minutes. Then stir gently with a wooden spoon. Cover and stand for a further 5 minutes.

SPICED PILAF
İç Pilav

10 portions

4 cups baldo rice
4 table spoons pinenuts
4 table spoons currants
250 gr. chicken or lamb liver
1 onion, medium
200 gr. butter
1 teaspoon pepper
salt
1 tea spoon allspice
5 cups water or meat stock
1 tea spoon sugar
1 bunch dill

PREPARATION

Pick over the rice and place into a bowl. Cover with hot water and add 1 tablespoon of salt. Stand for 30 minutes. Rinse in cold water several times and drain. Peel and dice the onions. Soak the currants in warm water until they swell, then drain. If using lamb liver, remove the fine membrane and wash (this is unnecessary for chicken liver). Chop the liver into tiny dice. Melt the butter in a saucepan and stir the pine nuts over the heat until lightly coloured. Add the chopped onion and when beginning to soften stir in the liver. Finally add the rice and stir with a wooden spoon over the heat for a few minutes. Stir in the currants and spices. Add the boiling water or stock, salt and sugar and stir once more. Cover and bring to boil over a high heat. Then cook over a low heat for about 15 minutes. When the liquid has evaporated and steam holes appear in the surface of the rice, remove from the heat. Stand for 10-15 minutes. Chop the dill finely and sprinkle over. Stir with a wooden spoon from the edges into the centre. Serve alonk or with meat dishes.

TOMATO PILAF
DOMATESLİ PİLAV

10 portions

3,5 cups baldo rice
salt
200 gr. butter
4 tomatoes
1 tea spoon sugar
5 cups water or meat stock

PREPARATION

Pick over the rice, add 1 tablespoon of salt and hot water to cover, and soak for 30 minutes. Rinse several times until the water runs clear. Drain. Peel the tomatoes, remove the seeds, and dice small. Melt the butter in a saucepan, add the tomatoes and cook until softened. Add the salt, sugar, water or stock and rice and stir once. Cover and when it boils reduce the heat. Cook over a low heat until the liquid evaporates and steam holes appear in the surface of the rice. Remove from the heat and set aside for 15 minutes. Stir the pilaf carefully from the sides inwards. Cover and stand for another 5 minutes before serving.

BULGUR PILAF

BULGUR PİLAVI

10 portions

1 kg. bulgur, coarse
200 gr. butter
4 onions, medium
10 bell peppers or green peppers, small
2 tomatoes, big
8 cups meat stock
salt
1/2 tea spoon pepper

PREPARATION

Pick over the bulgur, wash in plenty of water and drain. Dice the onion. Remove the stalks and seeds of the pepper, wash and chop finely. Peel the tomatoes, remove the seeds and chop small. Melt the butter in a saucepan, fry the onions until softened. Add the bulgur and stir over the heat with a wooden spoon for approximately 5 minutes. Add the tomato and pepper, stir for a few more minutes. Add the salt and black pepper then the boiling meat stock, stir and cover. Bring to the boil then lower the heat and cook until the liquid has evaporated and steam holes appear in the surface. Remove from the heat. Stand for 10-15 minutes. Stir with a wooden spoon from the sides inwards so that the grains separate. Cover and stand for another 5 minutes.

PILAF WITH ANCHOVIES
HAMSİLİ PİLAV

10 portions

500 gr. rice
1 kg. anchovies
4 cups water
2 onions
200 gr. butter
2 tablespoons mint
1/2 bunch dill
1 teaspoon pepper
1 teaspoon allspice
2 tablespoons currants
2 tablespoons pinenuts

PREPARATION

Pick over the rice and place in a bowl. Pour over enough hot water to cover and stir in 1 tablespoon salt. Set aside for 30 minutes. Rinse well in cold water until the water runs clear and drain. Soak the currants in warm water until they swell, then drain. Grease a circular oven dish well. Gut the anchovies and remove the heads and backbones. Wash, drain and sprinkle with salt. Arrange side by side skin side downwards in the base and cover the sides of the dish. Soften two chopped onions in melted butter, add the pinenuts and stir until lightly coloured. Add the rice and fry for 2-3 minutes. Add the mint, currants and 1 1/2 cups boiling water. Cover and wait until the rice absorbs the liquid. Add the allspice, black pepper and finally chopped dill and stir. Pour the pilaf into the oven dish, taking care not to disturb the anchovies. Lay remaining anchovies over the top, with the silvery skins upwards. Pour a cup of hot water over and bake in a pre-heated oven at 160°C for about 30 minutes. Turn out onto a serving plate and serve hot.

DESSERTS
TATLILAR

After accepting Islam in the 9th century, the Turks are celebrating a "Festival of Sweets" for three and a half days every year. As can be guessed from the name, during this festival, Turkish delights, marzipans, candy coated almonds, syrupy desserts and baklavas are swallowed by tired mouths in every house visited, and lots of soda is drunk.

Traditionally, guests present their hosts with desserts in Turkey. The idea stems from the philosopy "who eats sweet, talks sweet."

All towns have small dessert shops, namely muhallebici. Desserts may be classified into three groups: syrupy pastries, milk puddings and fruit desserts. Syrup is prepared by cooking water, sugar and lemon juice then poured onto baked pastry. Among syrupy pastries, baklava is worth mentioning. Baklava consists of fifteen layers, eight layers of pastry and seven layers of pistachio. Regionally filling may be varied with the substitution of hazelnuts or walnuts. Sekerpare, round pastry with a nut on top; vezir parmagi-finger of the vizier, shape of a finger; harem navels are interesting varieties.

Milk puddings are frequently cooked by housewives as they are simple to cook and light. Babies start nutrition with milk pudding muhallebi when their mothers cease to breast-feed them. Sutlac made with rice; dried apricots stuffed with clotted cream and nuts; red, jelly and pungent quince dessert are some examples. Syrupy desserts and fruit desserts may be eaten with clotted cream.Fruits are also used to make jams and compotes. There are some desserts made on religious occations. Noah's arc dessert and güllaç, thin sheets of pastry rested in milk are gifts of Islam to Turkey.

In Turkey, eat sweet, to talk sweet!

Baklava

MILK PUDDING WITH ROSE WATER
SU MUHALLEBİSİ

10 portions

10 cups milk
2 cups sugar
2 teaspoons salt
2 cups wheat starch
1/2 cup water
as much as desired rose water
powdered sugar, as desired
syrup as desired

PREPARATION

Place the milk, powder sugar and salt into a saucepan and bring to the boil. Dilute the wheat starch in 1/2 cup of water and whisk into the simmering milk, then stir constantly over a medium heat for at least 20 minutes until it thickens, making sure that the mixture does not catch. Wet a mould with sides at least 4 cm high, and pour the mixture in. Set aside to cool. Cut into squares and sprinkle powdered sugar and rose water over to serve. You may also serve with syrup.

Revani

BAKED RICE PUDDING
FIRINDA SÜTLAÇ

<u>10 portions</u>

6 table poons rice
4 cups water
4 egg yolks
10 cups milk
1 cup (200 gr) sugar
1 teaspoon crushed mastic
6 tablespoons (40 gr) wheat starch

PREPARATION
Pick over the rice, wash and drain. Add the rice to cold water, bring to
boil and simmer over a medium heat until the rice grains are tender.
Strain off the excess water. Blend the wheat starch with half a cup of
water. Crush the mastic with a little sugar in a mortar. In a separate
saucepan beat the egg yolks and stir in the milk. Add the sugar, mastic
and boiled rice, stir over a medium heat until the mixture comes to the
boil. Gradually stir in the diluted wheat starch. When the mixture starts
to bubble pour into ten ovenproof bowls. Place the bowls in a deep oven
tray and pour water into the tray to halfway up the sides of the bowls.
Bake in a pre-heated oven at 200°C until a brown skin has formed on top
for 25 minutes. Serve cold.

PUMPKIN DESSERT
KABAK TATLISI

10 portions

4,5 kg-half pumpkin
1 cup water
750 gr. sugar
200 gr. walnuts, shelled
250 gr. kaymak (clotted cream)

PREPARATION

Divide the pumpkin into four equal pieces, and cut away the stringy parts and seeds. Cut each piece into 4 again and finally in 4 lenghtways, and have pieces 10 cm long and 4 cm wide. Cut off the rind and the hard green parts below the rind. Wash and lay in a large saucepan. Pour the water and then the sugar over. Cover and cook over a low heat. Remove from heat when the syrup is thick. When cold, garnish with ground walnuts or kaymak.

SEMOLINA HELVA
İRMİK HELVASI

10 portions

2,5 cups (500 gr) semolina
5 cups milk
1 tablespoon pinenuts
250 gr. butter
2 cups sugar

PREPARATION

Tip the semolina and pine kernels into a large saucepan and cook over a very low heat for 30-45 minutes, stirring constatly with a wooden spoon until slightly coloured. Remove from the heat. Place the milk, butter and sugar in another saucepan and bring to boil over a medium heat, stirring continously with a wooden spoon. Gradually pour the boiling milk over the semolina and stir. Lower the heat and stirring continuously cook until the milk has all been absorbed. Then cover with a cloth, stir occasionally for 25 minutes. Serve warm or cold.

QUINCE DESSERT
AYVA TATLISI

10 portions

5 medium quinces
1 kg. sugar
1 lemon, squeezed
3 cloves
5 cups water
2 sour apples
100 gr. lohusa şekeri (optional) (a red sweet)
250 gr. Kaymak (clotted cream)

PREPARATION

Peel the quinces and divide in half. Cut out the core. Arrange in a shallow saucepan. Peel the apples and grate over the quinces. Sprinkle the sugar over, and add the water, lemon juice and cloves. If desired, crumble in the lohusa şekeri to color. Cover the pan with a lid or aluminum folio and cook over a gentle heat until the quinces are tender and the juice has thickened. Serve cold with kaymak (clotted cream).

Ekmek Kadayıfı

AŞURE

10 portions

400 gr wheat grains
125 gr. white beans
125 gr. chick peas
150 gr. dried apricots
200 gr. raisins
150 gr. dried figs
1 table spoon grated orange peels
800 gr. sugar
5 liters water
1 table spoon sunflower oil
1 cup milk
rosewater as desired

PREPARATION

Soak the wheat in warm water, the beans in cold water and the chickpeas in a warm salty water overnight. Drain the chickpeas and beans, rinse and place in separate saucepans. Add the cold water and bring to the boil. Cover and simmer until very tender. Drain. Remove the skins of the chickpeas. Chop the dried apricots and figs into hazelnut sized pieces. Pick off the stalks from the currants, wash and cover with water. Boil for 10 minutes and drain. Wash the wheat and drain. Place the wheat in a large saucepan with 5 litres of water and 1 tablespoon of sunflower oil. Bring to the boil, cover and simmer over a low heat, stirring occasionally to prevent catching. When the wheat is tender to the point of mushy, add the currants, and cook for a further 5 minutes, stirring occasionally. Stir in the grated orange peel, chickpeas and beans, stirring constantly. Simmer for another 5 minutes or so. Add the dried apricots and sugar.

APRICOTS WITH CLOTTED CREAM
KAYMAKLI KAYISI TATLISI

10 portions

350 gr. dried apricots
250 gr. sugar
2 1/2 cups water
250 gr. kaymak (clotted cream)
To decorate:
pistachionuts

PREPARATION

Soak the dried apricots in plenty of cold water overnight. Boil up the water and sugar to a syrup. Drain the apricots, place in the syrup and cook for at most 15 minutes. Set aside to cool. Split open the apricots, stuff with kaymak and close. Arrange on a service dish. Sprinkle whole or ground pistachio nuts over and serve.

SERAGLIO LOKMA
SARAY LOKMASI

1 cup water, 1/2 cup butter
1 teaspoon salt, 1 cup sifted flour
3 eggs, 1 cup margarine

PREPARATION

Boil water, add butter and salt, and stir until mixture boils. Turn flame low, add flour all at one time, stirring vigorously until mixture does not stick to the sides of the saucepan. Remove from heat. Add eggs one by one, beating thoroughly after each addition. Heat the margarine in a frying pan and drop the paste by spoonfuls into it. Fry until they become brown. Soften with syrup and serve cold.

SOUR CHERRY BREAD
VİŞNELİ EKMEK TATLISI

10 portions

1 package sliced toasts
1 kg. sour cherry
1 kg. sugar
5 cups water
1 pack ready-made cream

PREPARATION

Remove the crusts from the bread and cut into 2 cm slices. Divide each slice in half and lay them on a baking tray. Bake in a pre-heated oven at 150°C until lightly browned on both sides. Arrange in layers in a large shallow oven dish. Wash the cherries and remove the seeds. Place in a saucepan with water and sugar. Bring to the boil. Remove from the heat, and pour the cherries and juice over the bread. Allow to cool. Garnish with some of the sour cherries and cream.

SWEETENED DRY APRICOT STEW
KURU KAYISI HOŞAFI

PREPARATION

Soak the dried apricots overnight, and cook them the next day for 10 minutes with plenty of sugar. Make a thick syrup with extra sugar and the water in which the apricots were cooked, and pour it over the fruit. Chopped pistachios or other nuts and cream make this hoşaf even better.

YOGURT DESSERT
YOĞURT TATLISI

10 portions

6 eggs
3/4 cup (120 gr) sugar
1,5 cups (400 gr) yoghurt
1 1/4 cups (120 gr) flour
3/4 cups (120 gr) semolina
6 table spoons (40 gr) wheat starch
1 tea spoon baking powder
250 gr. kaymak (clotted cream)

for the syrup:
3.5 cups (750 gr) sugar
6 cups water
1/4 squeezed lemon

PREPARATION

Put the eggs and sugar in a bowl and place in a container of boiling water. Beat with a mixer or whisk until thickened. Mix the semolina and yogurt in a saucepan, place over a very low heat, and beat with a whisk until thick and smooth. Remove from the heat immediatly and continue to beat for a few more minutes. The mixture should not be allowed to boil. Combine the egg and yogurt mixtures. Slowly stir in the sieved flour, wheat starch and baking powder. İf wished you can add the grated zest of a small orange which gives a delicious aroma and flavour. Grease a baking tin (approximately 20 cm in diametre), pour in the mixture and spread evenly. Bake in a pre- heated oven at 180 (Cuntil the top turns a golden brown. Meanwhile put the ingredients for the syrup in a saucepan and boil for 2 minutes. Pour hot over the baked yogurt tatlısı as soon as you remove it from the oven. When cool cut in slices and garnish with kaymak (clotted cream), and strawberries.

CHICKEN BREAST PUDDING
TAVUK GÖĞSÜ

10 portions

2 lt. milk
350 gr. sugar
1 cup rice flour
4 chicken breasts
As much as desired cinnamon
1/4 cup chicken stock

PREPARATION

Add the riceflour to the milk and stir. Add the sugar and cook to pudding density.

Cook the chicken breasts, put into cold water and change the water every hour. The chicken smell will vanish in 4 hours. Chop small the chicken breasts, wash and simmer.

Take a big spoon of pudding, pour over the small chicken pieces and mash the pieces with the spoon. Add the mashed chicken to the pudding and bring to a boil. Add a cup of boiled milk, stir, cook until dense and remove from heat.

Pour the pudding into cups which are wet. Turn upside down when cold, remove from cups and serve with cinnamon.

Vezir Parmağı

CONTENTS